The Original
Summer Bridge
Activities™

3 to 4

W9-AZY-164

Teacher Recommended!

Carson-Dellosa Publishing LLC

P.O. Box 35665 • Greensboro, NC 27425 USA

carsondellosa.com

Caution: Exercise activities may require adult supervision. Before beginning any exercise activity, consult a physician. Written parental permission is suggested for those using this book in group situations. Children should always warm up prior to beginning any exercise activity and should stop immediately if they feel any discomfort during exercise.

Caution: Before beginning any food activity, ask parents' permission and inquire about the child's food allergies and religious or other food restrictions.

Caution: Nature activities may require adult supervision. Before beginning any nature activity, ask parents' permission and inquire about the child's plant and animal allergies. Remind the child not to touch plants or animals during the activity without adult supervision.

Caution: Before beginning any balloon activity, ask parents about possible latex allergies. Also, remember that uninflated or popped balloons may present a choking hazard.

The authors and publisher are not responsible or liable for any injury that may result from performing the exercises or activities in this book.

ISBN 978-1-62057-610-6

05-055141151

Table of Contents

About Summer Learning iv

About Summer Bridge Activities™ v

Skills Matrix vi

Encouraging Summer Reading viii

Summer Reading List ix

Section I: Monthly Goals and Word List 1

Introduction to Flexibility 2

Activity Pages 3

Science Experiments 43

Social Studies Activities 45

Outdoor Extension Activities 48

Section II: Monthly Goals and Word List 49

Introduction to Strength 50

Activity Pages 51

Science Experiments 91

Social Studies Activities 93

Outdoor Extension Activities 96

Section III: Monthly Goals and Word List 97

Introduction to Endurance 98

Activity Pages 99

Science Experiments 139

Social Studies Activities 141

Outdoor Extension Activities 144

Answer Key 145

Flash Cards

Certificate of Completion

About Summer Learning

Dear Parents:

Did you know that many children experience learning loss when they do not engage in educational activities during the summer? This means that some of what they have spent time learning over the preceding school year evaporates during the summer months. However, summer learning loss is something that you can help prevent. Below are a few suggestions for fun and engaging activities that can help children maintain and grow their academic skills during the summer.

- Read with your child every day. Visit your local library together and select books on subjects that interest your child.

- Ask your child's teacher to recommend books for summer reading.

- Explore parks, nature preserves, museums, and cultural centers.

- Consider every day as a day full of teachable moments. Measuring ingredients for recipes and reviewing maps before a car trip are ways to learn or reinforce skills.

- Each day, set goals for your child to accomplish. For example, complete five math problems or read one section or chapter in a book.

- Encourage your child to complete the activities in books such as Summer Bridge Activities™ to help bridge the summer learning gap.

To learn more about summer learning loss and summer learning programs, visit *www.summerlearning.org.*

Have a memorable summer!

Brenda McLaughlin and Sarah Pitcock
National Summer Learning Association

About Summer Bridge Activities™

Summer Bridge Activities™: Bridging Grades Third to Fourth prepares your rising fourth grader for a successful school year. The activities in this book are designed to review the skills that your child mastered in third grade, preview the skills that he or she will learn in fourth grade, and help prevent summer learning loss. No matter how wonderful your child's classroom experiences are, your involvement outside of the classroom is crucial to his or her academic success. Together with *Summer Bridge Activities™: Bridging Grades Third to Fourth*, you can fill the summer months with learning experiences that will deepen and enrich your child's knowledge and prepare your child for the upcoming school year.

Summer Bridge Activities™ is the original workbook series developed to help parents support their children academically during the summer months. While many other summer workbook series are available, Summer Bridge Activities™ continues to be the series that teachers recommend most.

The three sections in this workbook correspond to the three months of traditional summer vacation. Each section begins with a goal-setting activity, a word list, and information for parents about the fitness and character development activities located throughout the section.

To achieve maximum results, your child should complete two activity pages each day. Activities cover a range of subjects, including reading, writing, multiplication and division, grammar, and fitness. These age-appropriate activities are presented in a fun and creative way to challenge and engage your child. Each activity page is numbered by day, and each day includes a space for your child to place a colorful, motivational sticker after he or she completes the day's activities.

Bonus extension activities that encourage outdoor learning, science experiments, and social studies exercises are located at the end of each section. Complete these activities with your child throughout each month as time allows.

An answer key located at the end of the book allows you to check your child's work. The included flash cards help reinforce basic skills, and a certificate of completion will help you and your child celebrate his or her summer learning success!

Skills Matrix

Day	Addition & Subtraction	Character Development	Fitness	Geometry	Graphing & Probability	Language Arts & Writing	Measurement	Multiplication & Division	Numbers	Parts of Speech	Place Value	Prefixes & Suffixes	Problem Solving	Punctuation & Capitalization	Reading Comprehension	Science	Sentence Structure	Social Studies	Spelling	Vocabulary	Word Study
1	★					★									★						
2	★					★			★											★	
3	★					★						★									
4										★	★		★			★					
5	★									★					★						
6	★		★							★			★								
7									★		★			★							★
8	★																				★
9									★						★					★	
10	★			★											★			★			
11	★	★													★					★	
12					★				★						★						
13							★								★						★
14	★									★			★					★			
15	★									★			★							★	
16			★						★	★		★									
17										★					★						
18						★		★		★											★
19	★					★									★						
20	★							★	★												
									★	BONUS PAGES!						★		★			
1	★					★								★							
2				★						★					★					★	
3	★		★							★									★		
4				★		★														★	
5	★						★			★											
6								★		★										★	
7	★								★	★								★			
8			★	★			★	★													
9								★								★			★		
10	★					★				★			★								
11	★																			★	★

Skills Matrix

Day	Addition & Subtraction	Character Development	Fitness	Geometry	Graphing & Probability	Language Arts & Writing	Measurement	Multiplication & Division	Numbers	Parts of Speech	Place Value	Prefixes & Suffixes	Problem Solving	Punctuation & Capitalization	Reading Comprehension	Science	Sentence Structure	Social Studies	Spelling	Vocabulary	Word Study
12	★			★											★				★		
13				★								★			★						★
14	★					★														★	
15				★		★							★								★
16		★				★			★						★						
17							★			★					★						
18								★												★	
19	★							★	★											★	★
20							★								★				★		
BONUS PAGES!							★									★		★		★	
1	★				★										★						★
2			★				★								★						
3					★			★							★						
4					★			★	★				★								
5			★			★							★		★						
6						★									★					★	
7				★			★		★						★						
8				★											★						★
9				★		★								★							
10									★	★					★						
11	★	★				★															
12					★	★									★						
13						★			★											★	
14							★							★	★						
15				★		★	★										★				
16	★					★				★					★						
17	★													★	★			★			
18						★								★	★						
19	★				★	★		★						★							
20	★													★	★						
BONUS PAGES!							★									★		★			

vii

Encouraging Summer Reading

Literacy is the single most important skill that your child needs to be successful in school. The following list includes ideas of ways that you can help your child discover the great adventures of reading!

- Establish a time for reading each day. Ask your child about what he or she is reading. Try to relate the material to an event that is happening this summer or to another book or story.

- Let your child see you reading for enjoyment. Talk about the great things that you discover when you read.

- Create a summer reading list. Choose books from the reading list (pages ix–x) or head to the library and explore the shelves. A general rule for selecting books at the appropriate reading level is to choose a page and ask your child to read it aloud. If he or she does not know more than a few words on the page, the book may be too difficult.

- Read newspaper and magazine articles, recipes, menus, maps, and street signs on a daily basis to show your child the importance of reading.

- Find books that relate to your child's experiences. For example, if you are going camping, find a book about camping. This will help your child develop new interests.

- Visit the library each week. Let your child choose his or her own books, but do not hesitate to ask your librarian for suggestions. Often, librarians can recommend books based on what your child enjoyed in the past.

- Make up stories. This is especially fun to do in the car, on camping trips, or while waiting at the airport. Encourage your child to tell a story with a beginning, a middle, and an end. Or, have your child start a story and let other family members build on it.

- Encourage your child to join a summer reading club at the library or a local bookstore. Your child may enjoy talking to other children about the books that he or she has read.

Summer Reading List

The summer reading list includes fiction and nonfiction titles. Experts recommend that students entering the fourth grade read for at least 20 to 30 minutes each day. Ask your child questions about the story to reinforce comprehension.

Decide on an amount of daily reading time for each month. You may want to write the time on each Monthly Goals page at the beginning of each section.

Fiction

Ackerman, Karen
The Night Crossing

Baylor, Byrd
The Table Where Rich People Sit

Blume, Judy
Tales of a Fourth Grade Nothing

Catling, Patrick Skene
The Chocolate Touch

Cleary, Beverly
Beezus and Ramona
Ralph S. Mouse
Ramona Quimby, Age 8

Dahl, Roald
Fantastic Mr. Fox
James and the Giant Peach

Danziger, Paula
Amber Brown Is Not a Crayon

DeJong, Meindert
The Wheel on the School

Dowell, Frances O'Roark
Phineas L. MacGuire . . . Erupts:
The First Experiment

Eager, Edward
Half Magic

Frasier, Debra
Miss Alaineus: A Vocabulary Disaster

George, Jessica Day
Dragon Slippers

Graff, Lisa
The Thing About Georgie

Gregory, Kristiana
Across the Wide and Lonesome Prairie:
The Oregon Trail Diary of Hattie
Campbell, 1847

Griffin, Judith Berry
Phoebe the Spy

Laden, Nina
Bad Dog

Lansky, Bruce (ed.)
The Best of Girls to the Rescue: Tales of
Clever, Courageous Girls from
Around the World

Lobel, Arnold
Fables

Summer Reading List (continued)

Fiction (continued)

Low, William
Old Penn Station

MacDonald, Betty
Mrs. Piggle-Wiggle

Pennypacker, Sara
Clementine

Ringgold, Faith
Tar Beach

Schotter, Roni
The Boy Who Loved Words

Seuss, Dr.
Oh, the Places You'll Go!

Spyri, Johanna
Heidi

Steig, William
Dominic

Van Allsburg, Chris
The Garden of Abdul Gasazi

Waters, Kate
Samuel Eaton's Day: A Day in the Life of a Pilgrim Boy
Sarah Morton's Day: A Day in the Life of a Pilgrim Girl

Nonfiction

Arnosky, Jim
Field Trips

Bial, Raymond
A Handful of Dirt

Cherry, Lynne
Flute's Journey: The Life of a Wood Thrush
A River Ran Wild

Donald, Rhonda Lucas
Endangered Animals

Hooper, Meredith
The Pebble in My Pocket: A History of Our Earth

Lerner, Carol
Butterflies in the Garden

Locker, Thomas
Cloud Dance

Murawski, Darlyne A.
Spiders and Their Webs

Pratt, Kristin Joy
A Walk in the Rainforest

Rockwell, Anne
Why Are the Ice Caps Melting: The Dangers of Global Warming

St. George, Judith
So You Want to Be President?

Monthly Goals

A goal is something that you want to accomplish. Sometimes, reaching a goal can be hard work!

Think of three goals to set for yourself this month. For example, you may want to read for 20 minutes each day. Write your goals on the lines and review them with an adult.

Place a sticker next to each goal that you complete. Feel proud that you have met your goals!

1. _____   PLACE STICKER HERE

2. _____   PLACE STICKER HERE

3. _____   PLACE STICKER HERE

Word List

The following words are used in this section. They are good words for you to know. Read each word. Use a dictionary to look up each word that you do not know. Then, write two sentences. Use a word from the word list in each sentence.

briefly	exhibition
bronze	glacier
course	league
design	relief
displayed	represents

1. They relief my frend.

2. She 's briefly.

Introduction to Flexibility

This section includes fitness and character development activities that focus on flexibility. These activities are designed to get you moving and thinking about building your physical fitness and your character.

Physical Flexibility

For many people, being flexible means easily doing everyday tasks, such as bending to tie a shoe. Tasks like this can be hard for people who do not stretch often. Stretching will make your muscles more flexible. It can also improve your balance and coordination.

You probably stretch every day without realizing it. Do you ever reach for a dropped pencil or a box of cereal on the top shelf? If you do, then you are stretching. Try to improve your flexibility this summer. Set a stretching goal. For example, you might stretch every day until you can touch your toes.

Flexibility of Character

It is good to have a flexible body. It is also good to be mentally flexible. This means being open to change.

It can be upsetting when things do not go your way. Can you think of a time when an unexpected event ruined your plans? For example, a family trip to the zoo was canceled because the car had a flat tire. Unexpected events happen sometimes. How you react to those events often affects the outcome. Arm yourself with the tools to be flexible. Have realistic expectations. Find ways to make bad situations better. Look for good things that may come from disappointing events.

You can be mentally flexible by showing respect to other people. Sharing and accepting the differences of other people are also ways to be mentally flexible. This character trait gets easier with practice. Over the summer, practice and use your mental flexibility often.

Solve each problem.

The answers to addition problems are called ___total___ .

The answers to subtraction problems are called ___How many more___ .

1. $44 - 34 =$ ___10___
2. $25 + 23 =$ ___48___
3. $40 + 29 =$ ___69___
4. $50 - 15 =$ ___35___
5. $40 - 38 =$ ___2___
6. $12 + 15 =$ ___27___
7. $29 - 13 =$ ___16___
8. $23 + 23 =$ ___46___
9. $38 + 20 =$ ___58___
10. $17 - 5 =$ ___12___
11. $13 + 16 =$ ___29___
12. $26 + 43 =$ ___69___
13. $19 - 8 =$ ___11___
14. $39 - 27 =$ ___12___
15. $42 + 14 =$ ___56___
16. $28 - 5 =$ ___23___
17. $26 + 13 =$ ___39___
18. $51 + 27 =$ ___78___

Trace the letters in cursive.

Aa Bb Cc Dd Ee

Ff Gg Hh Ii Jj Kk

Ll Mm Nn Oo Pp

Qq Rr Ss Tt Uu Vv

Ww Xx Yy Zz

DAY 1

Read the passage. Then, answer the questions.

Glaciers

A glacier is a large, thick mass of ice. It forms when snow hardens into ice over a long period of time. It might not look like it, but glaciers can move. Glaciers usually move slowly. If a lot of ice melts at once, a glacier may **surge** forward, or move suddenly. Most glaciers are found in Antarctica (the continent at the South Pole) or in Greenland (a country near the North Pole). Areas with glaciers receive a lot of snowfall in the winter and have cool summers. Most glaciers are located in the mountains where few people live. Occasionally, glaciers can cause flooding in cities and towns. Falling ice from glaciers may block the path of people hiking on trails farther down the mountain. Icebergs are large, floating pieces of ice that have broken off from glaciers. Icebergs can cause problems for ships at sea.

19. What is the main idea of this passage?
    A. Icebergs can be dangerous to ships.
    B. Glaciers are large masses of ice found mainly in the mountains.
    C. People usually live far away from glaciers.

20. How does a glacier form? It form by a snow hardens into ice over a long period of time.

21. What does the word *surge* mean in this passage?
    A. move forward suddenly
    B. freeze into ice
    C. break off from an iceberg

22. Where are most glaciers located? In the mountains

23. What is the weather like where glaciers are found? cold

24. How can glaciers be dangerous? Ther darom are pointy

FACTOID: Glaciers store about 75% of Earth's freshwater.

4

Homophones are words that sound the same but have different meanings and are spelled differently. Write the correct homophone from the parentheses to complete each sentence.

1. I have _____two_____ more days of school. (to, two)

2. Have you _____read_____ this book before? (read, red)

3. That lion has large _____paws._____ . (paws, pause)

4. I like that song _____too_____ . (two, too)

5. The boys had _____to_____ much work to do before dark. (too, to)

6. _____Red_____ is my favorite color. (Red, Read)

7. We are going _____to_____ Lake Louise this summer. (to, two)

8. Please _____ the movie for a minute. (paws, pause)

Follow the directions.

9. Draw a square around the greatest number.

10. Count by 2s to 40. Underline the numbers you use.

11. Draw a triangle around the number that is 4 less than 62.

12. Draw an X over each odd number.

13. Circle all of the uppercase letters. Write the letters you circled in order, starting with the top row and moving left to right.

b	r	q	e	o	S	c	r	y	10	6	3
U	y	10	5	2	4	M	z	l	q	a	i
6	v	0	7	8	M	p	2	10	17	12	l
r	b	14	18	b	e	16	f	h	19	E	s
18	5	14	7	2	p	m	n	z	58	20	s
94	86	22	2	R	17	I	0	24	n	x	c
26	39	3	a	d	e	28	g	S	52	19	30
7	j	F	k	32	y	34	4	31	t	10	36
0	n	e	n	38	o	80	98	U	47	x	p
w	m	m	ll	N	3	14	39	c	r	e	t
q	u	v	9	7	6	w	5	40	w	13	19

_____

DAY 2

Use the fact family in each circle to make number sentences.

14.

⬭ 8
7 15

$15 + 8 = 23$

$15 + 7 = 22$

$15 - 8 = 7$

$15 - 7 = 6$

15.

⬭ 9
8 17

$17 + 9 = 26$

$17 + 8 = 25$

$17 - 9 = 8$

$17 - 8 = 7$

16.

⬭ 6
8 14

$14 + 8 = 22$

$14 + 6 = 20$

$14 - 8 = 6$

$14 - 6 = 4$

Trace the letters in cursive.

a a   c c   e e

m m   n n   o o

s s   r r   v v

x x   w w   u u

l l   t t   b b

FITNESS FLASH: Touch your toes 10 times.

* See page ii.

Add to find each sum.

1. 634
   + 268
   902

2. 987
   + 489
   1,766

3. 493
   + 277
   660

4. 888
   + 245
   1,123

5. 732
   + 299
   1,031

6. 947
   + 276
   1,223

7. 496
   + 394
   890

8. 557
   + 323
   880

9. 347
   + 254
   601

10. 665
    + 337
    1,002

Identify each sentence type. Write _D_ for declarative, _IN_ for interrogative, _E_ for exclamatory, or _IM_ for imperative.

11. __IN__ Whales have to eat a lot of food.

12. __D__ Why do you think that?

13. __E__ Whales are the largest animals living today.

14. __D__ Blue whales can weigh up to 200 tons each.

15. __IN__ They are gigantic!

16. __IM__ That is unbelievable!

17. __D__ Find out how much other animals eat.

18. __IN__ How much do lions eat?

19. __E__ They eat 50 or 60 pounds of meat daily.

20. __IN__ A lion can eat that much in one meal!

DAY 3

Read the story. Then, write the correct prefix in each blank. Use *dis-*, *in-*, *re-*, or *un-*.

My Uncle Paul worked in a bookstore. Uncle Paul always helped me find books to

read. He was never (21.) _dis_ pleased if I asked him for help. I (22.) _re_ call

the day I asked for a book about unsolved mysteries. Uncle Paul

(23.) _un_ covered some on the very top of the back shelf. They were dirty and

smelled dusty. They looked as if they had been (24.) _dis_ touched for years.

I started to read one. As I looked (25.) _un_ side, I noticed that some of the

pages were missing from the very end of the book. "Oh no!" I said. "This story is

(26.) _un_ complete. Now, I'll never know how it ends." I must have looked pretty

(27.) _dis_ appointed because Uncle Paul tried to cheer me up. He said, "I don't

mean to be (28.) _dis_ kind, but you wanted to read about unsolved mysteries. I think

you (29.) _re_ covered a real unsolved mystery!"

Read the paragraph. Then, write *fiction* or *nonfiction* on the line.

Army ants are one of the most feared types of ants. These ants are very destructive and can eat all living things in their paths. Army ants travel at night in groups of hundreds of thousands through the tropical forests of Africa and South America.

30. _fiction_

FACTOID: There are more than 10,000 known species of ants on Earth.

Solve each word problem.

1. I read 6 books in June. I read 3 books in July. I read 7 books in August. How many books did I read these three months? 16 books

2. Carla went on a weekend trip. She took 16 photos. She printed only 8 photos. How many photos did she not print? 8 Photos

3. I saw 12 birds on Monday. I saw 8 birds on Tuesday. I saw 7 birds on Wednesday. How many birds did I see in all? 27 birds

4. Sue counted 14 fish and 9 tadpoles in the pond. How many fewer tadpoles were there than fish? 13 tadpoles

Read each group of words. Write *S* if it is a sentence or *F* if it is a fragment.

5. _S_ Chris slid into home plate.

6. _S_ In the top row I.

7. _F_ Watched a squirrel.

8. _S_ The clown's funny hat fell off.

9. _F_ Pulled a wagon down.

10. _S_ In the forest, we saw three deer.

11. _F_ A plane landed at the airport.

12. _F_ Our team started to.

13. _F_ Mom broke a window when she was young.

DAY 4

Write each number.

EXAMPLE:

6 tens 8 ones ___**68**___	14. 9 tens 4 ones ___9 4___	15. 5 tens 0 ones ___5 0___	16. 10 tens 0 ones ___1 0 0___
17. 6 tens 3 hundreds 8 ones ___683___	18. 4 hundreds 0 tens 2 ones ___024___	19. 5 ones 6 hundreds 7 tens ___756___	20. 9 hundreds 3 ones 5 tens ___539___

An adjective is a word that describes a noun. Circle the adjective that describes each underlined noun.

21. Some prairie dogs live in large <u>communities</u> under the ground.

22. A mother prairie dog makes a nest of dried <u>plants</u> in the spring.

23. She gives birth to a litter of four <u>pups</u>.

24. She is a good <u>mother</u> and takes care of her pups.

25. The pups are ready to venture outside after six <u>weeks</u>.

26. The pups have many <u>friends</u>.

FITNESS FLASH: Do 10 shoulder shrugs.

* See page ii.

PLACE STICKER HERE

Read the passage. Then, answer the questions.

The Olympic Games

During the Olympic Games, people from all over the world gather to compete in different sporting events. The original Olympics were held in Greece around 776 BC. Athletes came together every four years to run races of different lengths. Those who won were given wreaths of olive branches. The modern Olympics were first held in 1896 in Greece. In 1994, the International Olympic Committee decided that the summer and winter Olympic Games should be held in different years. This means that every two years, thousands of people representing more than 200 countries come together to compete in either summer or winter sports. Today's top athletes receive gold, silver, or bronze medals and compete in hundreds of different events. The Olympics give each host country a chance to show its culture both to the people who come there and to the people who watch on TV. The sports may be different than in the original Olympics, but the spirit of goodwill and good sportsmanship is still the same.

1. What is the main idea of this passage?
    A. The Olympics are held every four years.
    B. People come to the Olympics from all over the world to compete in different sports.
    C. Today's top athletes receive gold, silver, or bronze medals.

2. When and where were the original Olympics held? _____

3. What did winners receive at the early Olympics?_____

4. How did the Olympics change in 1994?_____

_____

5. What do top Olympic athletes receive today?_____

6. How do the Olympics help people learn about different cultures? _____

_____

DAY 5

Add to find each sum.

7. 24
    41
    + 32

    47

8. 91
    28
    + 13

    132

9. 35
    66
    + 37

    138

10. 22
    61
    + 84

    267

11. 16
    10
    + 31

    57

12. 45
    32
    + 48

    125

13. 45
    52
    + 21

    118

14. 28
    39
    + 21

    88

15. 27
    65
    + 85

    77

16. 74
    26
    + 39

    139

Write the correct forms of each adjective.

		Adjectives That Compare Two Nouns	Adjectives That Compare More Than Two Nouns
EXAMPLE:	long	*longer*	*longest*
17.	soft	sofeter	sofest
18.	large	larger	largest
19.	flat	flater	flatst
20.	sweet	sweeter	sweeetst
21.	wide	wider	widest
22.	cool	cooler	coolst

CHARACTER CHECK: Look up the word *considerate* in a dictionary. Then, think of two ways that you can be considerate.

Add to find each sum.

1.　3.76
　　+ 2.66
　　6.42

2.　3.49
　　+ 2.33
　　5.82

3.　8.78
　　+ 2.87
　　11.65

4.　4.36
　　+ 2.96
　　7.32

5.　3.48
　　+ 9.48
　　12.96

6.　4.98
　　+ 4.39
　　9.37

7.　4.77
　　+ 2.98
　　7.65

8.　3.96
　　+ 4.74
　　8.70

9.　9.01
　　+ 1.09
　　10.10

10.　8.34
　　+ 2.49
　　10.83

The Athletic Advantage

There are a lot of benefits to stretching. Do you like basketball, dancing, or another physical activity that requires you to move, run, or jump? If so, then you should try to improve your flexibility. Whatever your favorite physical activity is, set a goal for yourself to complete at least one stretch every day that will help make you a better athlete. For example, if you like tennis and want to improve your backhand, practice a trunk-twist stretch at least twice a day. As with all stretching exercises, start slowly. Gradually increase your stretching as you become more flexible. This is how professional athletes improve their abilities. So, stretch for better performance!

* See page ii.

DAY 6

Write different ways to make the amount of money in each problem. Use real money to help you.

EXAMPLE:

10¢ **10 pennies**

2 nickels

1 nickel, 5 pennies

1 dime

11. $1.00   4 quater

12. 25¢
25 Pennies

13. $1.60
4 quater and 60. Pennies

A noun names a person, a place, or a thing. An action verb tells what a noun is doing. Circle the nouns. Underline the verbs.

elephant	sang	ate	fixed
laugh	tent	Mr. Chip	team
book	California	guitar	landed
Lake Street	cleaned	yell	played
visited	Kent	write	strength
engine	jump	broccoli	leap

FACTOID: Saturn is the only planet in our solar system that could float on water.

Write each number.

1.   five hundred sixty-one ___561___

2.   eight hundred ___800___

3.   four hundred eighty-six ___486___

4.   one hundred fifty ___150___

Count how many are in each set. Write each number.

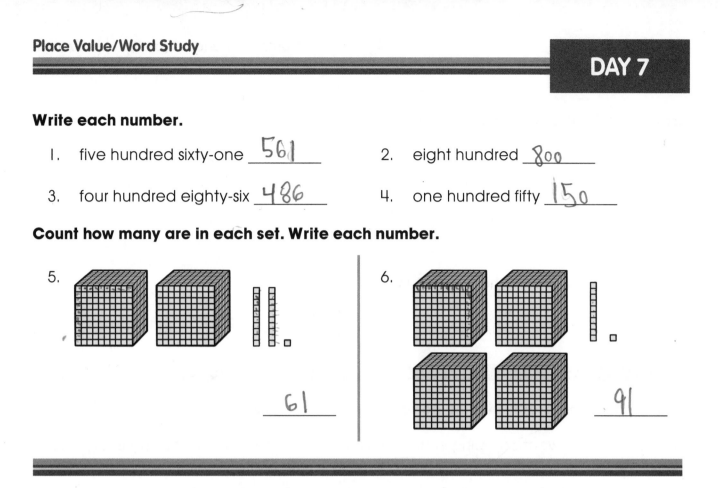

5.   ___61___

6.   ___91___

A compound word is made of two words that have been put together to make a new word. Use the words from the word bank to make a compound word that matches each description.

bath	team	horse	back	scare	pine
apple	storm	snow	tub	mates	crow

EXAMPLE:

a place where you can go to get clean ___*bathtub*___

7.   a fruit with spiky skin ___Pine___

8.   what farmers put in cornfields to scare birds away ___Scare___

9.   a type of weather event that some places get in the winter ___Storm___

10.   if you ride on a horse, you have this kind of ride ___horse___

11.   people who play on a team with you ___team___

DAY 7

Round each number to the nearest 10.

EXAMPLE:

28 = **30**   12. 85 = 90   13. 13 = 20   14. 44 = 50

15. 33 = 40   16. 92 = 100   17. 78 = 80   18. 18 = 20

Round each number to the nearest 100.

19. 767 = 770   20. 841 = 850   21. 211 = 220   22. 587 = 590

Rewrite the paragraph with the correct punctuation and capitalization.

last summer we went camping in colorado we went hiking and swimming every day one time i actually saw a baby white-tailed deer with spots we also took photos of a lot of pretty rocks flowers and leaves we had a great time i didn't want to leave

Last sumer we went camping in colorado we went hiking a swimming every day one time I actually saw a baby white-tailed deer with spots we also took photos of a lot of pretty rocks, flowers, and leaves we had a great time I didn't whant to leave.

FITNESS FLASH: Practice a V-sit. Stretch five times.

* See page ii.

Add to find each sum.

1. 57
42
+ 33
132

2. 38
46
+ 23
107

3. 17
36
+ 22
75

4. 85
36
+ 74
195

5. 76
23
+ 67
176

6. 56
21
+ 32
109

7. 39
48
+ 59
146

8. 45
23
+ 54
122

9. 24
51
+ 76
151

10. 25
45
+ 56
126

11. 55
21
+ 37
112

12. 33
30
+ 36
99

Negative words usually have _no_ or _not_ in them. Avoid using two negative words in the same sentence. Underline the second negative word in each sentence. Then, write a positive word to replace the word you underlined.

Negative	Positive	Negative	Positive
no, none	a, any, one	no one	anyone, someone
nothing	anything, something	nobody	anybody, somebody
nowhere	anywhere, somewhere	never	ever

13. There are no flamingos living nowhere near me. _nothing_

14. Can't nobody tell me where they live? _a, any, one_

15. There are not no other wading birds as big and colorful. _No, None_

16. I will not never forget the day that I saw my first flamingo. _never_

17. There must not be nothing else like flamingos. _anything, something_

DAY 8

Circle the word in each row that is divided correctly into syllables.

18. (cact/us)   ca/ctus   (cac/tus)   c/actus

19. (bli/ster)   blist/er   blis/ter   bl/ister

20. (al/ways)   (a/lways)   alw/ays   alwa/ys

21. har/bor   ha/rbor   harb/or   harbo/r

22. fl/ower   (flo/wer)   flowe/r   flow/er

23. bas/ket   bask/et   ba/sket   baske/t

24. obe/ys   (o/beys)   ob/eys   obey/s

Write the abbreviation for each word.

EXAMPLE:

December ___*Dec.*___   25. Wednesday ___Wed___

26. January ___Jan___   27. August ___Aug___

28. Sunday ___Sun___   29. Thursday ___Thu___

30. February ___Feb___   31. September ___Sep___

32. Monday ___Mon___   33. Friday ___Fri___

34. March ___Mar___   35. October ___Oct___

36. Tuesday ___Tue___   37. Saturday ___Sat___

38. April ___Apr___   39. November ___Nov___

FACTOID: The first roller coaster in the United States opened in 1884 in Coney Island, New York.

Compare each set of numbers. Write < (less than) or > (greater than) on each line.

1. 126 __>__ 261

2. 999 __<__ 899

3. 126 __>__ 226

4. 342 __<__ 231

5. 524 __<__ 624

6. 524 __>__ 624

7. 619 __>__ 719

8. 267 __<__ 367

9. 580 __<__ 579

10. 1,638 __<__ 738

11. 4,206 __>__ 5,206

12. 3,487 __<__ 3,748

Synonyms are words that mean about the same thing. Complete each sentence with a word from the word bank that is a synonym for the underlined word.

~~silent~~	~~tip~~	~~lid~~	~~mistake~~	~~small~~	~~happy~~	~~tug~~	tear

13. Dan's pencil <u>point</u> was dull, so he had to sharpen the ___tip___ .

14. The <u>top</u> came off of the ant farm, but I quickly replaced the ___mistake___ .

15. The <u>cheerful</u> girl was very ___happy___ when she got an A on her science project.

16. Anna got a <u>rip</u> in her jeans, so her mother repaired the ___tear___ .

17. Gina had to <u>pull</u> and ___tug___ the heavy chair to move it.

18. Dana was <u>quiet</u> because her mother asked her to be ___silent___ while the baby slept.

19. I made an <u>error</u>, and the teacher showed me my ___lid___ .

20. The <u>tiny</u> earring was hard to find because it was so ___small___ .

DAY 9

Read the passage. Then, answer the questions.

Harriet Tubman

Harriet Tubman was a brave woman. She grew up as a slave in Maryland. As an adult, she escaped north to Pennsylvania. Tubman returned to Maryland to help rescue her family. She returned many times to help other slaves. She guided slaves to safety along a network known as the Underground Railroad. People who helped slaves move to freedom were called "conductors." They were named after the people who controlled trains on railroads. In 1861, the United States began fighting the Civil War. This war was partly a struggle between northern and southern states over whether people should be allowed to own slaves. President Abraham Lincoln signed a law in 1863. The law stated that slavery was no longer allowed in the United States. With the law on her side, Tubman continued for many years to help people who were treated unfairly.

21. What is the main idea of this passage?
    A. "Conductors" were people who helped slaves move to freedom.
    B. Harriet Tubman lived in Maryland.
    C. Harriet Tubman helped people on the Underground Railroad.

22. Why did Tubman return to Maryland? To help other pepole in Maryland.

23. What was the Underground Railroad? _____

_____

24. What did conductors on the Underground Railroad do? _____

_____

25. What was the Civil War? _____

_____

FITNESS FLASH: Do arm circles for 30 seconds.

* See page ii.

PLACE STICKER HERE

Add to find each sum.

| 1. | 376 + 266 | 2. | 349 + 233 | 3. | 878 + 287 | 4. | 436 + 296 | 5. | 948 + 348 | 6. | 498 + 439 |

| 7. | 477 + 298 | 8. | 474 + 396 | 9. | 901 + 109 | 10. | 834 + 249 | 11. | 499 + 292 | 12. | 118 + 953 |

Use commas, add words, and remove or rearrange words to combine the sentences.

EXAMPLE:

I like my friends Wendy and Pete. I also like Mandy and Joe.

I like my friends Wendy, Pete, Mandy, and Joe.

13. Dogs and cats can be pets. Gerbils and hamsters can be pets too.

_____

_____

14. I am wearing blue jeans and a striped shirt. My shoes are black, and my socks are green. On my head is a baseball cap.

_____

_____

DAY 10

Write the name of each shape.

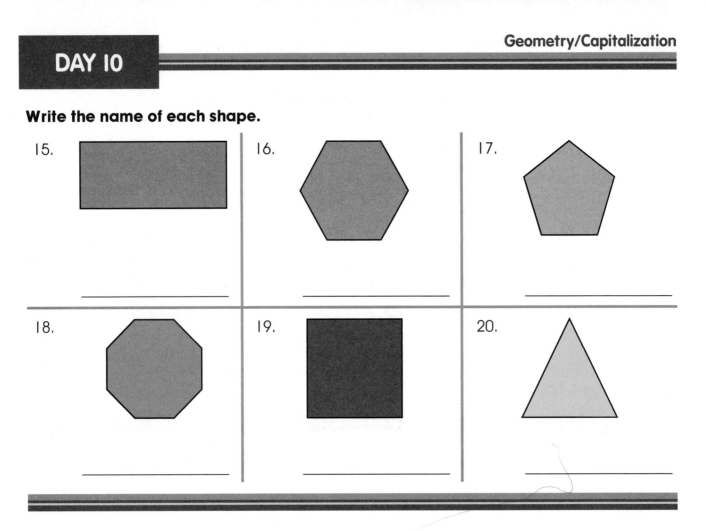

15. _____

16. _____

17. _____

18. _____

19. _____

20. _____

Draw three lines beneath each letter that should be capitalized.

Pocahontas

pocahontas was an American Indian who lived in virginia during the time of the first

english settlement of america. According to legend, pocahontas saved the life of

captain john smith. Later, she moved to jamestown and took the name rebecca. She

married mr. john rolfe, and they traveled to england to meet king james. pocahontas

died in england and was buried there. She had one son, thomas.

CHARACTER CHECK: Write five ways that you can show respect to your family members and friends, animals, and the earth.

PLACE
STICKER
HERE

Write the word from the word bank that matches each description.

knead	sense	praise	certain
wheat	purchase	numb	guide

1. unable to feel _____

2. we do this to dough _____

3. sure of something _____

4. to buy something _____

5. to see, hear, feel, taste, or smell _____

6. flour is made from this _____

7. a leader of a group _____

8. to express approval _____

Compassion Collage

Compassion is seeing that someone needs help or understanding and offering him support. Create a compassion collage. Think about ways that people show compassion. Cut out compassion pictures and words from magazines and newspapers. Use markers, poster board, and glue to create your collage. Draw small pictures, write words, and add stickers to the collage. Give your collage a title, such as *The C's of Compassion: Care, Concern, Consider*. Display the collage so that others can see how you have captured compassion.

© Carson-Dellosa

Add to find each sum.

9.	566 + 467	10.	979 + 354	11.	945 + 379	12.	888 + 276	13.	871 + 739

14.	655 + 478	15.	675 + 597	16.	456 + 327	17.	347 + 254	18.	493 + 349

Draw three lines beneath each letter that should be capitalized.

july 1, 2010

dear aunt Laura,

Thank you so much for the gift card! I'm going to use it to buy a game i've been

wanting. When you and uncle Mike come to visit this summer, we can all play my new

game together.

your nephew,

Blake

FACTOID: Rain has never been recorded at the center of Chile's Atacama Desert.

PLACE
STICKER
HERE

Divide each set of objects into the correct number of groups.

EXAMPLE:

Make 3 equal groups.

How many are in each group? **7**

1. Make 5 equal groups.

    How many are in each group? _3_

2. Make 2 equal groups.

    How many are in each group? _8_

3. Make 4 equal groups.

    How many are in each group? _2_

Add commas where they belong in each sentence.

EXAMPLE:

August 10, 1970, and May 10, 1973, are birth dates in our family.

4. My parents were married in Portland Oregon on May 1 1999.

5. We had chicken potatoes corn gravy and ice cream for dinner.

6. George Washington became the first U.S. president on April 30 1789.

7. Sam was born on June 16 1947 in Rome Italy.

8. We saw deer bears elk and goats on our trip.

9. On July 24 1962 in Boise Idaho I won the big race.

DAY 12

Multiply to find each product.

10.	26 × 12	11.	49 × 33	12.	87 × 28	13.	51 × 42	14.	94 × 78

15.	81 × 32	16.	23 × 18	17.	55 × 37	18.	62 × 29	19.	75 × 46

Present-tense verbs describe what is happening now. Past-tense verbs describe what happened in the past. Write a verb to complete each sentence. If there is an *n* beside the line, write a present-tense verb. If there is a *p* beside the line, write a past-tense verb.

20. Two dogs (p) _____ down the road.

21. The wind (n) _____ and the trees (n) _____ .

22. We can (n) _____ and (n) _____ in the race.

23. Last night, I (p) _____ past your house.

24. I (p) _____ at the jokes on TV last night.

25. Yesterday, we (p) _____ tulips and roses.

FITNESS FLASH: Practice a V-sit. Stretch five times.

* See page ii.

PLACE STICKER HERE

Complete each sentence by writing *more than*, *less than*, or *equal to*.

2 cups = 1 pint	2 pints = 1 quart	4 quarts = 1 gallon

1. 2 pints are _____ 1 quart.

2. 1 gallon is _____ 1 pint.

3. 1 pint is _____ 1 quart.

4. 6 pints are _____ 3 quarts.

5. 3 quarts are _____ 1 gallon.

6. 2 pints are_____ 4 cups.

7. 3 cups are _____ 1 quart.

8. 8 quarts are _____ 2 gallons.

Write the correct word from the word bank to answer each question.

night	hopped	baby	pear
different	dry	knock	

9. Which word begins with a silent letter? _____

10. Which word has the *t* sound at the end, but the letter *t* is not making the sound?

_____

11. Which word has a silent *gh*? _____

12. Which word has the long *e* sound but does not include the letter *e*?

_____

13. Which word has three syllables?_____

14. Which word sounds the same as *pair*? _____

15. Which word ends with the long *i* sound? _____

DAY 13

Read the passage. Then, answer the questions.

Roberto Clemente

Roberto Clemente was born in Puerto Rico in 1934. He played baseball in his neighborhood as a child. Then, he played for his high school team. He joined a junior national league when he was 16. He played baseball briefly in Canada before signing to play for the Pittsburgh Pirates in 1954. Clemente served in the U.S. Marine Reserves for several years. That helped him grow stronger physically. He helped the Pirates win two World Series. During the off-season, Clemente often went back to Puerto Rico to help people. He liked visiting children in hospitals to give them hope that they could get well. An earthquake hit the country of Nicaragua in 1972. At age 38, Clemente died in an airplane crash on his way to deliver supplies to Nicaragua. He was elected to the Baseball Hall of Fame in 1973. He was the first Hispanic player to receive that honor.

16. What is the main idea of this passage?
    A. Roberto Clemente was a great baseball player who also helped people.
    B. Roberto Clemente died in an airplane crash.
    C. Roberto Clemente was elected to the Baseball Hall of Fame.

17. Where was Clemente born? _____

18. Where in the United States did Clemente play baseball? _____

19. What did Clemente do during the off-season? _____

20. What happened in Nicaragua in 1972? _____

    _____

21. Why was Clemente flying to Nicaragua? _____

    _____

FACTOID: The rules of modern baseball were originally called the Knickerbocker Rules.

PLACE STICKER HERE

Solve each word problem.

1. How many days are between the 18th and 28th day of the month?

2. Tony is next to last in line. He is also 10th from the 1st person in line. How many people are in line?

3. If today is June 22, what date will it be 1 week from today?

4. Jack is 16th in line. How many people are ahead of him?

The subject of a sentence is whom or what the sentence is about. The predicate of a sentence tells something about the subject. Both can have one or more words. Circle the subject and underline the predicate of each sentence.

EXAMPLE:

(Our team) won the game.

5. We went on a picnic.

6. A little red fox ran past us.

7. Some birds make nests for their eggs.

8. Clowns make me laugh.

9. The king rode a bike.

10. April lost her house keys.

11. Lee auditioned for the school play.

12. We started to swim.

13. The frog hopped onto the lily pad.

14. Lions live in groups called prides.

15. Olivia's mom baked the pie.

16. Noah worked in his garden.

17. I finished the book yesterday.

18. Mom and I rode our horses.

19. My brother went to the park.

DAY 14

Subtract to find each difference.

20.	62 − 19	21.	27 − 18	22.	45 − 38	23.	73 − 19	24.	42 − 29

25.	19 − 9	26.	86 − 57	27.	66 − 59	28.	44 − 26	29.	33 − 17

Write the correct present-tense form of the verb _be_ to complete each sentence.

30. Mona _____ my next door neighbor.

31. You _____ a great friend.

32. I _____ the oldest in my family.

33. Bill and Shelby_____ at the movies.

34. I _____ at my aunt's house.

35. You _____ very helpful today.

36. Pizza _____ my favorite food.

FITNESS FLASH: Touch your toes 10 times.

* See page ii.

PLACE STICKER HERE

Solve each word problem. Show your work.

1. Taylor's mom volunteered at the face-painting booth. She started with 14 tubes of face paint. At the end of the festival, she had 7 tubes left. How many tubes did she use during the festival?

2. Sean scored 5 baskets in the free throw contest. His friend Joshua scored 9 baskets. How many more baskets did Joshua score than Sean?

3. Twelve teachers sat in the dunking booth to raise money for new library books. Nine of them were dunked. How many teachers were not dunked?

4. At the end of the festival, Alexis noticed that she had 2 tickets left. If she started the festival with 10 tickets, how many tickets did she use?

Circle the word that does not belong in each group of words. Then, describe why the other words belong together.

5. tuba, clarinet, jazz, flute, harp _____

6. tire, hammer, screwdriver, wrench _____

7. robin, hawk, sparrow, dog, crow _____

8. Moon, Mars, Earth, Jupiter, Venus _____

9. lettuce, peach, carrot, peas, beets _____

10. rose, daisy, lazy, tulip, lily _____

DAY 15

Solve each problem.

11. 6.34
    − 2.68

12. 9.87
    + 4.89

13. 4.93
    − 2.77

14. 8.88
    + 2.76

15. 7.32
    − 2.99

16. 2.76
    + 9.47

17. 3.94
    + 4.96

18. 5.57
    − 3.23

19. 2.54
    + 3.47

20. 6.65
    − 3.37

Complete each sentence with the future-tense form of the verb in parentheses.

21. Maria _____ dinner tonight.

    (cook)

22. Angelo _____ his stepmother this weekend.

    (visit)

23. Carrie _____ to the movies tomorrow.

    (go)

24. Scott _____ his new book this evening.

    (read)

25. Wendy _____ me her new bracelet when she returns.

    (show)

CHARACTER CHECK: Think of a time when you did something nice for a friend or family member. How did this make you feel?

PLACE STICKER HERE

Add a suffix to each word. Use -est, -tion, or -ty. Double, drop, or change some letters if needed.

EXAMPLE:

tasty _tastiest_   1. sad _____

2. act _____   3. direct _____

4. safe _____   5. dirt _____

6. hungry _____   7. invent _____

8. prepare _____   9. happy _____

10. heavy _____   11. honest _____

The words _is_ and _are_ tell that something is happening now. Use _is_ with singular subjects and _are_ with plural subjects. Write _is_ or _are_ to correctly complete each sentence.

12. Max and I _____ best friends.

13. Bill _____ visiting his grandparents this week.

14. We _____ going camping at the lake.

15. Megan _____ biking with her friend Toni.

16. Her sister _____ in the eighth grade.

17. Those bananas _____ very ripe.

18. That book _____ one of my favorites.

19. Hugo and Malia _____ bringing snacks to the party.

DAY 16

Write the numbers in order from greatest to least.

20.   261   325   496   547   _____ _____ _____ _____

21.   746   793   733   779   _____ _____ _____ _____

22.   596   579   488   499   _____ _____ _____ _____

23.   496   649   964   946   _____ _____ _____ _____

Write the numbers in order from least to greatest.

24.   764   674   746   647   _____ _____ _____ _____

25.   503   530   353   550   _____ _____ _____ _____

26.   940   579   488   499   _____ _____ _____ _____

27.   496   649   964   946   _____ _____ _____ _____

Catch and Stretch

Did you know that a backyard game of catch can improve your flexibility? Find a friend or family member and a variety of balls, such as a tennis ball, baseball, softball, or foam ball. Throw each ball back and forth. As you throw, concentrate on extending your front foot and throwing arm. As this gets easier, increase the distance between you and your partner. For a challenge, try throwing with your other hand. This will be harder, but it will give both sides of your body equal stretching time. As you throw, remember to "stretch" your limits!

FACTOID: Nepal is the only country to have a national flag that is not a rectangle.

* See page ii.

PLACE STICKER HERE

Read the story. Then, write four details from the story in the order that they occurred.

Quinn and Phillip washed their dad's car. First, they filled a bucket with soapy water. Quinn got some old rags from the house while Phillip got the hose. They put soapy water all over the car and wiped off the dirt. Next, they rinsed the car with water. To finish the job, Quinn and Phillip dried the car with some clean towels. They were both surprised when their dad gave them $5 each.

1. _____

2. _____

3. _____

4. _____

Each word below contains the suffix -est, -tion, or -ty. Circle each suffix. Then, write the base word.

EXAMPLE:

safe(ty) _____*safe*_____

5. saddest _____

6. hungriest _____

7. preparation _____

8. invention _____

9. tasty _____

10. certainty _____

11. loyalty _____

12. direction _____

13. suggestion _____

14. loveliest _____

15. surest _____

Read the passage. Then, answer the questions.

Lucy Maud Montgomery

Lucy Maud Montgomery is famous for creating the character of Anne Shirley in the Anne of Green Gables series. Montgomery was born in 1874 on Prince Edward Island in Canada. She lived with her grandparents and went to class in a one-room schoolhouse. Her first poem was published when she was 17 years old. She wrote *Anne of Green Gables* in 1905, but it was not published until 1908. The book became a best-seller, and Montgomery wrote several other books based on the main character. Two films and at least seven TV shows have been made from the Anne of Green Gables series. Although Montgomery moved away from Prince Edward Island in 1911, all but one of her books are set there. Many people still visit the island today to see where Anne Shirley grew up.

16. What is the main idea of this passage?
    A. Lucy Maud Montgomery grew up on Prince Edward Island.
    B. Lucy Maud Montgomery is famous for writing *Anne of Green Gables*.
    C. Lucy Maud Montgomery was a schoolteacher.

17. Who is Anne Shirley? _____

18. What was Montgomery's early life like? _____

    _____

19. When was Montgomery's first poem published? _____

20. How can you tell that *Anne of Green Gables* was a popular book?

    _____

21. Why do many people visit Prince Edward Island today?

    _____

FITNESS FLASH: Do arm circles for 30 seconds.

* See page ii.

PLACE STICKER HERE

Multiply to find each product.

1. 16
    × 5

2. 15
    × 7

3. 28
    × 3

4. 24
    × 4

5. 26
    × 4

6. 47
    × 2

7. 19
    × 4

8. 19
    × 5

9. 38
    × 2

10. 45
    × 4

Write the past-tense form of each underlined verb.

11. A tadpole <u>hatches</u> from an egg in a pond. _____

12. He <u>looks</u> like a small fish at first. _____

13. The tadpole <u>uses</u> his tail to swim. _____

14. He <u>breathes</u> with gills. _____

15. His appearance <u>changes</u> after a few weeks. _____

16. He <u>starts</u> to grow hind legs. _____

17. His head <u>flattens</u>. _____

18. His gills <u>vanish</u>. _____

19. His tail <u>disappears</u>. _____

20. He <u>hops</u> onto dry land. _____

DAY 18

Get a dictionary. Choose any page between 40 and 55. Then, follow the directions.

21. Write the guide words for that page. _____

22. Write the meaning of the guide word that is on the right. _____

_____

23. How many syllables does your guide word have? _____

24. What mark is used to show how words are divided into syllables? _____

25. Guide words show the _____ and the _____ words on the page.

Clipped words are short versions of longer words. Write the clipped word for each underlined word.

EXAMPLE:

Upton ate a hamburger and fruit for lunch. _____ *burger* _____

26. When Ryan grows up, he wants to fly airplanes. _____

27. A hippopotamus can hold her breath for a long time. _____

28. Have you ever been inside a submarine? _____

29. Lori loves talking with her grandmother on the telephone. _____

30. Matt was amazed by the photograph in the art gallery. _____

FACTOID: If the sun were hollow, it could hold more than one million Earths inside it.

PLACE STICKER HERE

Read the passage. Then, answer the questions.

Elisha Otis

Have you ever ridden in an elevator? Elevators make it much easier for people to get from one floor to another in a tall building. At one time, elevators were not as safe as they are today. Elisha Otis helped change that. Early elevators used ropes that sometimes broke, sending the people riding the elevator to the ground. To make elevators safer, Otis made wooden guide rails to go on each side of an elevator. Cables ran through the rails and were connected to a spring that would pull the elevator up if the cables broke. Otis displayed his invention for the first time at the New York Crystal Palace Exhibition in 1853. His safety elevators were used in buildings as tall as the Eiffel Tower in Paris, France, and the Empire State Building in New York City, New York. Otis died in 1861. His sons, Charles and Norton, continued to sell his design, and many elevators today still have the Otis name on them.

1. What is the main idea of this passage?
    A. The Otis family still sells elevators today.
    B. At one time, elevators were unsafe to use.
    C. Elisha Otis found a way to make elevators safe.

2. Why were early elevators dangerous? _____

    _____

3. What did the spring in Otis's elevators do? _____

    _____

4. When and where was Otis's elevator displayed for the first time?_____

5. What are two buildings that used Otis's elevator design? _____

    _____

6. What did Otis's sons do after his death? _____

    _____

DAY 19

Subtract to find each difference.

7. 64
    − 57

8. 23
    − 9

9. 70
    − 23

10. 43
    − 14

11. 63
    − 45

12. 91
    − 42

13. 38
    − 19

14. 81
    − 15

15. 55
    − 9

16. 82
    − 16

Fill in the blanks to complete the friendly letter. Use correct capitalization.

_____ (date)

_____ , (greeting)

I'm having a _____ summer. So far, the best part of the summer has been

_____

_____

_____

_____ , (closing)

_____ (your name)

FITNESS FLASH: Do 10 shoulder shrugs.

* See page ii.

PLACE STICKER HERE

40

A

Add to find each sum.

1.	3,878	2.	9,651	3.	3,981	4.	76	5.	34
	4,981		3,321		2,357		59		67
	+ 8,165		+ 2,283		+ 4,652		+ 53		+ 24

6.	776	7.	5,349	8.	676	9.	7,028	10.	6,048
	453		3,274		734		4,354		3,278
	+ 719		+ 7,184		+ 651		+ 5,684		+ 5,328

Read each verb. Write *A* if it is a present-tense action verb. Write *L* if it is a linking verb.

EXAMPLE:

	A	bloom		**L**	is
11.	_____	has	12.	_____	hatch
13.	_____	have	14.	_____	appears
15.	_____	pretend	16.	_____	stir
17.	_____	becomes	18.	_____	study
19.	_____	walk	20.	_____	hold
21.	_____	were	22.	_____	am
23.	_____	skip	24.	_____	was

DAY 20

Divide to find each quotient.

25. 2)84   26. 2)62   27. 2)68   28. 3)93

29. 7)70   30. 5)55   31. 3)69   32. 9)99

33. 3)36   34. 9)90   35. 3)42   36. 4)80

Read each pair of sentences. Circle the letter of the sentence that shows future tense.

37. A. Mischa ran to the market.
    B. Mischa will run around the block.

38. A. I am having green beans with dinner.
    B. I will have corn tomorrow.

39. A. Troy will catch the ball.
    B. Troy catches the ball.

40. A. He will go to the new school.
    B. He went to the new school.

41. A. Davion washed the dog.
    B. Davion will wash the dog.

CHARACTER CHECK: What qualities are important for a friend to have?

42

PLACE STICKER HERE

Coffee Filter Chromatography

How can colors be separated?

Chromatography is a process used to separate colors. This activity shows how part of the ink in water-soluble markers can be dissolved. Other, more soluble colors will travel up a coffee filter with water.

Materials:
- 3 water-soluble markers (not permanent markers)
- drinking glass
- ruler
- coffee filter
- masking tape
- scissors
- water

Procedure:

Pour water into the glass so that it is about a half-inch (1.3 cm) deep. Label each glass and marker *1*, *2*, or *3* using masking tape and the markers. Cut the coffee filter into three strips, one for each marker. Use the water-soluble markers to make one large dot one-third of the way up each coffee filter strip. Do this for all three markers. Place each coffee filter strip in the glass with the same number as the marker. The ink dots should be near, but not under, the water. Let the strips absorb the water.

1. What happened to the ink dots as the coffee filter strips absorbed water?

    _____

2. What happened differently to each of the three different ink dots? _____

    _____

    _____

3. Which marker's ink traveled the highest on a coffee filter strip? List the other markers in order from highest to lowest. _____

    _____

BONUS

Speed Racer

How is the height of a ramp related to the speed of a toy?

Kinetic energy is the energy of motion. Potential energy is stored energy, or the energy of position.

Materials:

- ruler
- toy car
- stopwatch
- wooden ramp of any size

Procedure:

Raise one end of the ramp to the lowest height (about 1.5 inches [4 cm]) required for the toy car to roll from one end to the other. Place the car at the top of the ramp and use the stopwatch to time it as it rolls to the bottom of the ramp. Record the speed of the car and the height of the ramp on the chart below. Repeat the activity two more times, raising the height of the ramp each time.

Trial	Height	Time
1		
2		
3		

1. What is the relationship between the height of the ramp and the speed of the object? _____

2. What surfaces might cause the toy car to roll faster or slower? _____

_____

3. Try another object, such as a golf or tennis ball. What happens to the speed of the object if it has more mass? _____

Prime Lines

Lines of longitude are imaginary lines that run north to south on a map. They are marked in degrees (°) and help us find locations around the world. The prime meridian is the line at 0° longitude. The lines of longitude on a map are measured in 15° segments from the prime meridian. Places east of the prime meridian have the letter *E* after their degrees. Places west of the prime meridian have the letter *W* after their degrees.

Study the map. Then, answer the questions.

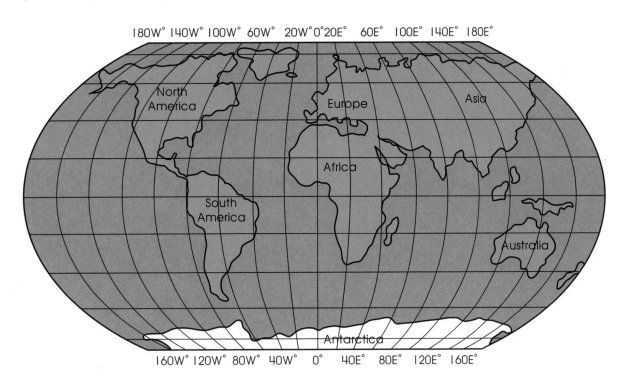

1. The prime meridian is at _____ ° longitude.

2. For locations in South America, the longitude should be followed by the letter

    _____ .

3. For locations in most of Africa, the longitude should be followed by the letter

    _____ .

4. Use an orange crayon or marker to trace the prime meridian.

BONUS

Map Scale

A map scale represents distance on a map. A map cannot be shown at actual size, so it must be made smaller to fit on paper. On the map below, 1 cm = 100 kilometers.

Study the map of Egypt. Measure the distance between dots with a ruler. Then, change the centimeters to kilometers to find the actual distance between each pair of cities.

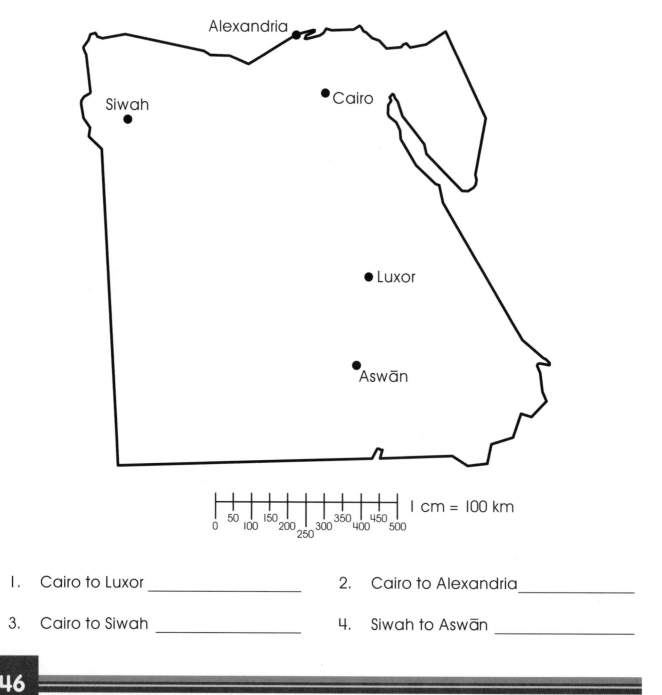

1. Cairo to Luxor _____

2. Cairo to Alexandria_____

3. Cairo to Siwah _____

4. Siwah to Aswān _____

Using a Map

Write the letter of the physical feature next to its name. Use an atlas if you need help.

1. _____ Rocky Mountains

2. _____ Great Lakes

3. _____ Rio Grande

4. _____ Atlantic Ocean

5. _____ Great Salt Lake

6. _____ Great Basin

7. _____ Mississippi River

8. _____ Appalachian Mountains

9. _____ Sierra Nevada Mountains

10. _____ Pacific Ocean

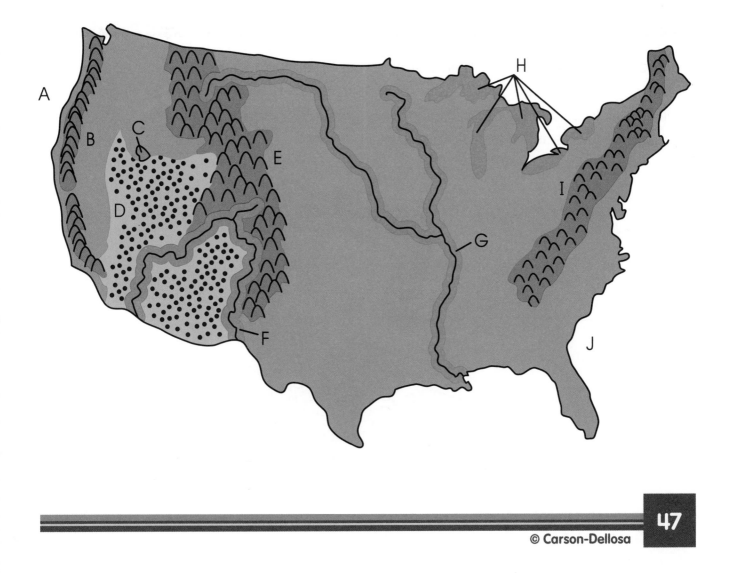

Take It Outside!

Turn your backyard or neighborhood into a math classroom to practice estimation. Put on your gardening gloves and pick up a small clump of grass, wood chips, pine straw, or other safe, small material. Estimate how many pieces are in the group. Then, place the material on the ground and count the number of pieces in it to see how close your estimate was.

Make a relief map of an outdoor space near your home. Wear gardening gloves and use sand, mud, sticks, and other natural materials to form the physical features of the area. Shape the land features on a hard, flat surface, such as a piece of plywood or a sandbox floor. Some of the physical features may not be the usual ones found in your social studies class. Make whatever features are noticeable on the landscape's surface, such as hills, driveways, ponds, and playground equipment.

Gather a variety of natural objects, such as shells, stones, leaves, small sticks, pine straw, and bark. Use glue to attach the objects to a flat, square piece of wood or cardboard to create a natural masterpiece. Make a shape, design, or even a scene to illustrate the beauty of the natural world.

* See page ii.

Monthly Goals

Think of three goals to set for yourself this month. For example, you may want to learn five math facts each week. Write your goals on the lines and review them with an adult.

Place a sticker next to each goal that you complete. Feel proud that you have met your goals!

1. _____
   PLACE
   STICKER
   HERE

2. _____
   PLACE
   STICKER
   HERE

3. _____
   PLACE
   STICKER
   HERE

Word List

The following words are used in this section. They are good words for you to know. Read each word. Use a dictionary to look up each word that you do not know. Then, write two sentences. Use a word from the word list in each sentence.

astronomy	description
choosing	improve
coordinate	instant
degrees	recreation
demanding	scattered

1. _____

   _____

2. _____

   _____

Introduction to Strength

This section includes fitness and character development activities that focus on strength. These activities are designed to get you moving and thinking about strengthening your body and your character.

Physical Strength

Like flexibility, strength is necessary for you to be healthy. You may think that a strong person is someone who can lift a lot of weight. However, strength is more than the ability to pick up heavy things. Strength is built over time. You are stronger now than you were in kindergarten. What are some activities that you can do now that you could not do then?

You can gain strength through everyday activities and many fun exercises. Carry grocery bags to build your arms. Ride a bike to strengthen your legs. Swim to strengthen your whole body. Exercises such as push-ups and chin-ups are also great strength builders.

Set goals this summer to improve your strength. Base your goals on activities you enjoy. Talk about your goals with an adult. As you meet your goals, set new ones. Celebrate your stronger, healthier body!

Strength of Character

As you build your physical strength, work on your inner strength too. Having a strong character means standing up for who you are, even if others do not agree with your point of view.

You can show inner strength in many ways, such as being honest, standing up for someone who needs your help, and putting your best efforts into every task. It is not always easy to show inner strength. Can you think of a time when you used inner strength to handle a situation, such being teased by another child at the park?

Improve your inner strength over the summer. Think about ways you can show strength of character, such as having good sportsmanship in your baseball league. Reflect on your positive growth. Be proud of your strong character!

Add to find each sum.

1.	238 + 348	2.	349 + 233	3.	434 + 948	4.	869 + 572	5.	458 + 749
6.	638 + 422	7.	539 + 468	8.	396 + 578	9.	955 + 134	10.	367 + 984

Write a book report about your favorite book. Use the outline to help you.

Title _____

Author _____

Main characters _____

Where and when does the story take place? _____

What is the main idea of the book? _____

_____

Why did you like the book? _____

_____

_____

DAY 1

Quotation marks set off what someone says. Write quotation marks in each sentence around what each person says.

EXAMPLE:

Uncle Neil said, "I will pack a picnic lunch."

11. Where is the big beach ball? asked Jeff.

12. Ilene exclaimed, That is a wonderful idea!

13. Come and do your work, Grandma said, or you can't go with us.

14. Yesterday, said Ella, I saw a pretty robin in the tree by my window.

15. I will always take care of my pets, promised Theodore.

16. Rachel said, Maybe we should have practiced more.

17. Dr. Jacobs asked, How are you, Pat?

On a separate sheet of paper, write a story about a real or imaginary place you would like to visit this summer.

Consider the following questions before you begin to write.

- Who are the characters in the story?

- Where does the story take place?

- How does the story begin?

- What happens next?

- How does the story end?

FACTOID: Humans have kept dogs as pets for about 10,000 years.

PLACE STICKER HERE

Answer each question about the coordinate grid.

1. Which shape is located at (5,3)?

   _____

2. At which coordinate is the square located? _____

3. Circle the shape located at (3,4).

4. Draw a line to connect the shapes located at (4,1) and (1,5).

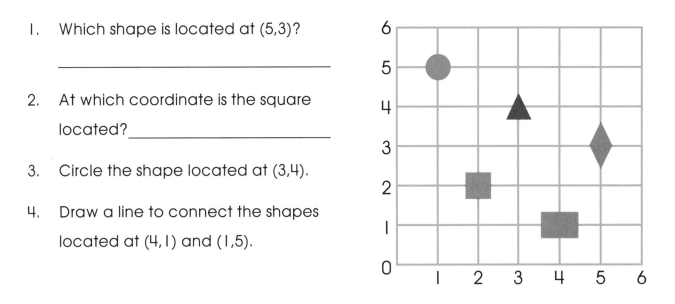

Common nouns are general names for people, places, or things. Proper nouns name specific people, places, or things and begin with uppercase letters. Write each noun under the correct heading.

	Common Nouns	**Proper Nouns**
dog	_____	_____
Monday		
ocean	_____	_____
Main Street		
class	_____	_____
November		
holiday	_____	_____
Mr. Brown		
July	_____	_____
boat		
beans	_____	_____
Rex		
apple	_____	_____
North Carolina		

DAY 2

Read the passage. Then, answer the questions.

Choosing a Pet

Before you decide what kind of pet you would like to own, there are some things you should think about. First, find out how much care the pet will need. Dogs need to be walked; horses need to be exercised; cats need a place to scratch. All pets need to be kept clean and well fed. You should also think about where your pet would live. Big pets need a lot of room while little pets do not need as much room.

5. What is the topic of the passage?
   A. caring for a dog
   C. feeding big pets

   B. choosing a pet
   D. where pets live

6. What is the main idea?
   A. finding good homes for pets
   C. things to think about before choosing a pet

   B. things to do when choosing a pet
   D. bring your pet home

Write the correct homophone from the word bank to complete each sentence.

too	two	to	cent	scent	sent

7. The _____ kittens played with the ball.

8. A penny equals one _____ .

9. My aunt asked me to go _____ the store.

10. Malcolm _____ a letter to his friend.

11. I will clean my desk and the table _____ .

12. The flower has a sweet _____ .

FITNESS FLASH: Do 10 lunges.

* See page ii.

PLACE STICKER HERE

Solve each problem.

1. 7.42
    − 1.16

2. 8.70
    − 6.30

3. 3.69
    − 1.25

4. 9.60
    + 1.92

5. 575
    − 162

6. 600
    + 197

7. 804
    + 129

8. 133
    − 124

9. 202
    − 102

10. 623
    + 527

Circle the articles *a*, *an*, and *the* in the sentences. Then, underline the noun that each article modifies.

11. Our dog sleeps in a bed.

12. The movie made us laugh.

13. I carried an umbrella in the rain.

14. Our boat had a leak.

15. Earth rotates around the sun.

16. I ate an apple and a sandwich for lunch.

17. Dad keeps the nails in an egg carton.

18. The books filled the shelf.

19. Rick saw a blue whale in the ocean.

20. The elephant likes to eat peanuts.

DAY 3

Read each group of words. Circle each correctly spelled word and write it on the line.

21. wunderful   wonderful   wondirful   _____

22. warm   wirm   warme   _____

23. wurried   woried   worried   _____

24. woh   hwo   who   _____

25. wair   where   wher   _____

26. weigh   weh   wiegh   _____

27. wint   wat   want   _____

28. w'ont   won't   wo'nt   _____

Tug-of-War Trials

Play tug-of-war. Tie several sturdy pieces of fabric together to make a "rope." Be sure to use a red piece of fabric in the middle. Use a ruler or other straight object to place a line on the ground. Group a few friends or family members into teams. Have each team member get ready at her rope position. Then, have them start pulling on the rope at the same time until one team pulls the other across the line. Change the teams. When everyone is done showing her strength, celebrate as a group with refreshing glasses of lemonade.

FACTOID: The U.S. Library of Congress has about 650 miles (1,046 km) of bookshelves.

* See page ii.

Name each figure by its points and label it with the correct symbol.

EXAMPLES:

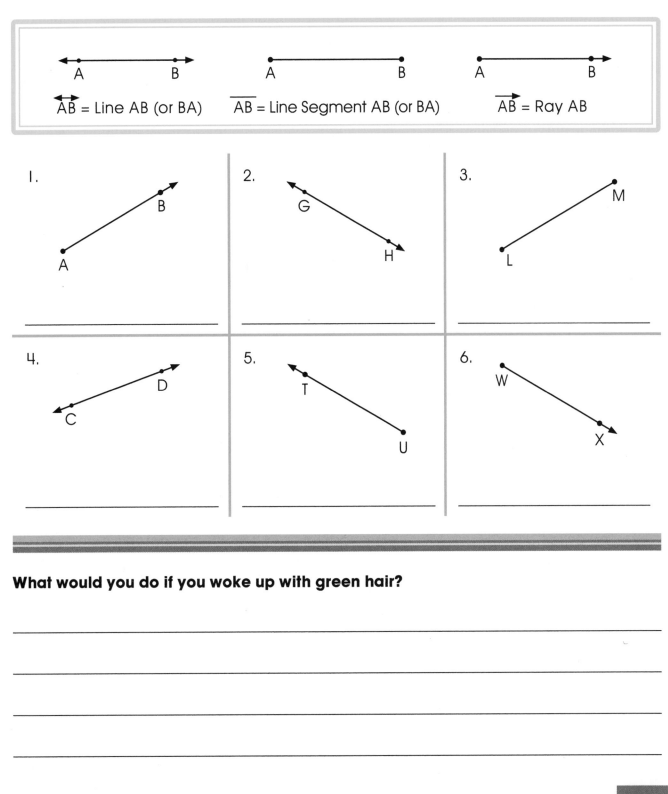

Below the figures:

1.

_____

2.

_____

3.

_____

4.

_____

5.

_____

6.

_____

What would you do if you woke up with green hair?

_____

_____

_____

_____

DAY 4

Write the correct homophone from the parentheses to complete each sentence.

7. Jennifer has two _____ and three oranges. (pears, pairs)

8. Brian can never _____ to play the game right. (seam, seem)

9. Mother will sift the _____ for the cookies. (flour, flower)

10. I hope that I can get everything _____ on time. (write, right)

11. Nannette _____ the baking contest. (won, one)

12. The bread _____ was very sticky. (doe, dough)

Context clues are the words around a word you do not know. Use context clues to figure out the meaning of each underlined word. Then, circle the letter next to the word's correct meaning.

13. My brother and I often <u>argue</u> about who gets to use the computer.
    A. work   B. disagree   C. study

14. The <u>official</u> told us not to enter the building until 8 o'clock.
    A. person in charge   B. nurse   C. child

15. Josie saw an <u>unusual</u> light in the sky and asked her father what it was.
    A. dark   B. star   C. different

16. The <u>cardinal</u> in my backyard is a beautiful sight. I love his bright red color and sweet song.
    A. singer   B. branch   C. bird with red feathers

17. Mom asked me to turn down the <u>volume</u> on the TV because it was too loud.
    A. noise level   B. book   C. color

 FITNESS FLASH: Do five push-ups.

* See page ii.

PLACE STICKER HERE

Use the clock to answer each question.

1.   What time does the clock show?

   _____

2.   How long does it take for the minute
   hand to move from 6 to 5?

   _____

3.   What time will it be when the minute hand reaches 12? _____

4.   What time will it be when the minute hand moves 15 minutes? _____

Write the correct article to complete each sentence.

5.   I enjoyed watching _____ game.

6.   Would you like _____ egg salad sandwich?

7.   I have _____ dog and _____ cat.

8.   Did you hear _____ thunder?

9.   An eagle flew over _____ tree.

10.   My grandmother gave me _____ new bike.

11.   The wind blew my umbrella down _____ street.

12.   Mrs. Hayes said that I did _____ good job on my art project.

13.   Was there _____ egg in the bird's nest?

DAY 5

Add to find each sum.

| 14. | 4,340
5,433
+ 3,238 | 15. | 356
674
+ 380 | 16. | 54
39
+ 73 | 17. | 634
198
+ 518 | 18. | 67
98
+ 74 |

| 19. | 47
34
+ 99 | 20. | 321
436
+ 548 | 21. | 2,783
2,546
+ 6,748 | 22. | 9,418
8,009
+ 7,245 | 23. | 4,259
1,564
+ 2,873 |

An adverb is a word that modifies a verb. Circle the adverb in each sentence. Then, underline the verb that the adverb modifies.

24. On Independence Day, we usually go to the parade.

25. We drive slowly because of traffic.

26. The parade often begins with a marching band.

27. The marching band plays loudly.

28. The huge crowd cheers excitedly.

29. My favorite part is when the big floats pass near us.

30. All of the floats are decorated beautifully.

31. We never see one we don't like.

CHARACTER CHECK: Think about an area in your life that you would like to improve. Set a goal for yourself.

Complete each multiplication chart.

1.

× **2**	
4	
8	
3	6
6	
9	
5	10
7	

2.

× **3**	
3	9
7	
5	
2	
6	18
4	
8	

3.

× **4**	
10	
5	20
8	
4	
7	
6	
9	

4.

× **5**	
9	
2	
6	
3	15
5	
7	
4	

Write the correct word from the word bank to complete each sentence.

cottage
quarter
curtains
circus
bell
pictures
pennies
market
chatter

5. Look at all of the funny _____ in this book.

6. You can buy bread and milk at the _____ .

7. We live in a small _____ .

8. This pencil costs a _____ .

9. I am saving a lot of _____ in a jar.

10. The clowns at the _____ were great.

11. When you hear the _____ , run fast.

12. We have white _____ on our windows.

13. Chipmunks _____ .

DAY 6

Divide to find each quotient.

14. $6\overline{)36}$ 15. $8\overline{)40}$ 16. $4\overline{)48}$ 17. $7\overline{)63}$

18. $8\overline{)56}$ 19. $7\overline{)35}$ 20. $9\overline{)72}$ 21. $7\overline{)28}$

Write the correct past-tense form of the irregular verb in parentheses to complete each sentence.

22. Our teacher _____ our class a book about insects. (read)

23. I _____ Mr. Lee before he was my teacher. (know)

24. Ms. Kemp _____ us that we could eat outside today. (tell)

25. Drew _____ that I can borrow his jump rope anytime. (say)

26. I _____ a bird chirping in a tree. (hear)

27. Cody _____ a new baseball glove today. (buy)

28. Hannah _____ her favorite blue shirt under her bed. (find)

29. Brooke and Gene each _____ an apple for a snack. (eat)

30. Jaime and her dad _____ a bookcase for her room. (build)

FACTOID: The largest recorded prairie dog town was located in Texas. It covered about 25,000 square miles (65,000 square kilometers).

PLACE STICKER HERE

Draw a straight line through three numbers that, when added together, total each sum provided.

1. Sum: 78

20	28	14
16	32	42
19	18	13

2. Sum: 110

16	33	64
39	22	44
51	10	72

3. Sum: 251

71	47	18
82	20	46
98	43	33

4. Sum: 149

15	93	24
63	25	33
63	25	61

5. Sum: 506

94	100	90
88	206	58
79	200	96

6. Sum: 189

94	100	90
88	20	58
79	10	96

Write the correct past- or present-tense form of the verb in parentheses to complete each sentence.

7. My friends and I like to _____ clay animals. (make)

8. Yesterday, we_____ the clay into different shapes. (roll)

9. Jeremy _____ making a clay hippo yesterday. (enjoy)

10. Our teacher _____ us bake the clay animals. (help)

11. He always _____ them in the kiln. (place)

12. After they were baked and cooled, we _____ them. (paint)

13. Often, we _____ them as gifts. (give)

DAY 7

Read each group of words. Write the words in the correct order to make complete sentences. Use correct punctuation and capitalization.

14. rode hill the I down on bike a _____

_____

15. garden a our mom backyard I planted and in my _____

_____

16. themselves elephant animals when braced all the sneezed the of _____

_____

17. bottles of full wagon a pulled cory _____

_____

18. book went I bed closed and my to _____

_____

Continue each counting pattern.

19.	0	3	6	9	12	___	___	___	24	___
20.	6	12	18	24	___	___	___	48	___	___
21.	12	16	20	24	___	___	___	___	44	
22.	33	30	27	24	___	___	___	9	___	
23.	100	98	96	94	___	___	___	86	___	___

FITNESS FLASH: Do 10 sit-ups.

* See page ii.

PLACE STICKER HERE

Temperatures are measured in degrees Fahrenheit (°F) and degrees Celsius (°C). Thirty-two degrees Fahrenheit is equal to 0 degrees Celsius. Write the temperature shown on each thermometer.

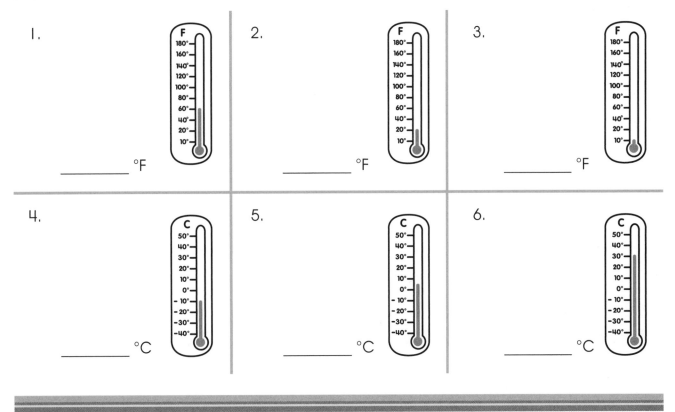

1. _____ °F

2. _____ °F

3. _____ °F

4. _____ °C

5. _____ °C

6. _____ °C

Each side of a geometric solid is called a face. Write the number of faces for each solid.

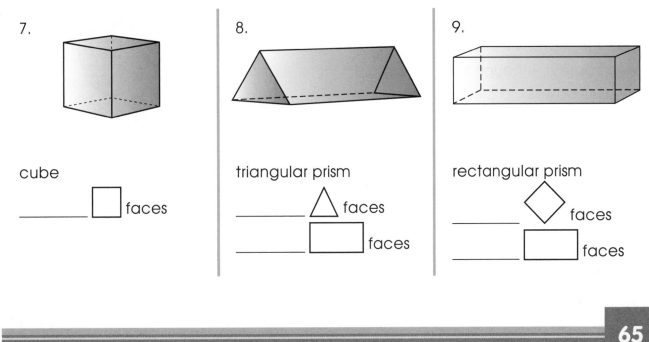

7. cube

_____ faces

8. triangular prism

_____ faces

_____ faces

9. rectangular prism

_____ faces

_____ faces

DAY 8

Divide to find each quotient.

10. $2\overline{)34}$ 11. $7\overline{)56}$ 12. $7\overline{)49}$ 13. $5\overline{)5}$

14. $9\overline{)45}$ 15. $4\overline{)36}$ 16. $9\overline{)36}$ 17. $5\overline{)35}$

18. $9\overline{)27}$ 19. $8\overline{)32}$ 20. $6\overline{)66}$ 21. $8\overline{)16}$

Demanding Up-Downs

There are many great exercises to improve your strength. One that uses your entire body is called an up-down. Begin by running in place. Then, drop to the ground with your chest to the floor and your legs straight behind you. Do one push-up. Then, jump back to your feet and run in place again. Remember to start slowly. Although it is not easy, doing up-downs is a great way to improve your overall fitness.

FACTOID: Cheetahs are the only cats that do not have fully retractable claws.

* See page ii.

PLACE STICKER HERE

Answer each question.

1. How many 6s are in 18? _____

2. How many 9s are in 18? _____

3. How many 5s are in 25? _____

4. How many 7s are in 21? _____

5. How many 2s are in 8? _____

6. How many 8s are in 32? _____

7. How many 4s are in 20? _____

8. How many 6s are in 36? _____

Read each sentence. If the underlined word is spelled correctly, write *correct*. If it is spelled incorrectly, rewrite the word with the correct spelling.

9. I'd like a glass of water. _____

10. Do you know where they've been today? _____

11. Be carefull with that knife. _____

12. My mom was very unhappy today. _____

13. What did Joni plant in her gardin? _____

14. We looked at all of the babyies in the hospital. _____

15. Aunt Mary canned 10 pounds of cherries. _____

16. He waved at us from the window. _____

17. Did you like the new movee? _____

18. Remember to set your alarm clock. _____

Read the story. Then, answer the questions.

Good Friends

Robert and Kaye are two of my best friends. We have gone to school together since we were in kindergarten. We even go to summer camp and the recreation center together. There are many reasons why I like to spend time with them. Robert always lets me borrow his skateboard. He knows that if I had a skateboard, I would let him borrow it. Robert is a person I can count on too. When we are out riding our bikes together, Kaye sometimes lets me ride in front while she rides behind me. She understands that one way to be a good friend is by taking turns and being fair.

19. How is Robert a good friend? _____

_____

20. Is Kaye a fair person? Why? _____

_____

21. List three things that the friends do together. _____

_____

22. Write a few sentences about what you think makes a good friend.

_____

_____

_____

_____

FITNESS FLASH: Do 10 squats.

* See page ii.

PLACE STICKER HERE

Solve each word problem. Show your work.

1. Nancy's dog weighs 63 pounds. Janet's dog weighs 54 pounds. How many pounds do the two dogs weigh altogether?

2. Jake collected 694 marbles. Joyce collected 966. How many fewer marbles did Jake collect than Joyce?

3. Reid threw 259 balls. Kirk threw 137 balls. How many more balls did Reid throw than Kirk?

4. Sasha has 42 cards. She divides them into 6 equal stacks. How many cards are in each stack?

Read each pair of words. For each pair, write one way the two things are alike and one way they are different.

5. leopard, cheetah _____

_____

6. keyboard, piano _____

_____

7. cabin, tent _____

_____

8. whistle, sing _____

_____

DAY 10

Subtract to find each difference.

9. 943
   − 549

10. 7,452
    − 6,789

11. 526
    − 268

12. 526
    − 498

13. 754
    − 528

14. 751
    − 439

15. 8,236
    − 5,548

16. 7,840
    − 4,251

17. 6,324
    − 3,489

18. 7,223
    − 1,759

Write the missing form of each irregular verb. Use a dictionary if needed.

present	past	past with *has* or *have*
19. sing	_____	has or have sung
20. tell	told	has or have _____
21. bring	_____	has or have brought
22. wear	wore	has or have _____
23. take	_____	has or have taken

CHARACTER CHECK: Look up the word *responsibility* in a dictionary. Then, write three ways that you can be responsible.

PLACE STICKER HERE

Add to find each sum.

1.	6,898	2.	8,459	3.	525	4.	5,265	5.	2,147
	5,433		4,908		653		2,278		3,255
	+ 2,154		+ 4,356		+ 896		+ 8,365		+ 2,256

6.	654	7.	7,092	8.	5,768	9.	4,265	10.	8,214
	452		5,405		6,937		5,124		7,716
	+ 138		+ 6,124		+ 7,034		+ 6,489		+ 6,389

Write the plural form of the underlined word to complete each sentence.

11. The <u>wolf</u> howled until two more _____ howled with him.

12. She put that book on the top <u>shelf</u> and all of the other books on the bottom

    _____ .

13. The horse has a special horseshoe on its chipped <u>hoof</u> and regular horseshoes

    on its other _____ .

14. The <u>child</u> played alone until the other _____ came.

15. His <u>wife</u> talked with some other _____ at the meeting.

16. Did you see the yellow <u>leaf</u> in that pile of _____ ?

DAY 11

Solve each problem.

| 17. | 4,936
 + 5,432 | 18. | 9,675
 − 4,283 | 19. | 5,349
 + 6,393 | 20. | 6,434
 − 6,398 | 21. | 754
 − 528 |

| 22. | 751
 − 439 | 23. | 8,236
 − 5,548 | 24. | 7,840
 − 4,251 | 25. | 6,324
 − 3,489 | 26. | 7,223
 − 1,759 |

Use the words from the word bank to solve the crossword puzzle.

Across

27. very sure

28. to make something look larger

29. to go behind

30. something that needs to be done now

31. to care for the sick

Down

32. to spin

33. to send back

34. not better

Word bank:
urgent   positive   nurse   worse
return   magnify   follow   twirl

FACTOID: Adult white-tailed deer can run up to 30 miles (48 km) per hour.

PLACE STICKER HERE

Add to find each sum.

1. 38.78
    + 84.56

2. 96.75
    + 42.83

3. 32.34
    + 46.52

4. 89.00
    + 39.57

5. 92.31
    + 53.32

6. 85.69
    + 25.46

7. 74.58
    + 54.94

8. 23.43
    + 73.28

9. 48.02
    + 36.89

10. 74.87
    + 58.26

Write the letter of each definition next to the correct geometry term.

11. _____ parallel lines

12. _____ perpendicular lines

13. _____ vertex

14. _____ face

15. _____ edge

16. _____ ray

17. _____ line segment

18. _____ angle

19. _____ intersecting lines

A. a line with one endpoint that continues in one direction

B. the endpoint of three line segments on a solid figure

C. a flat surface of a solid figure

D. where two or more faces of a solid figure meet

E. lines that intersect to form four right angles

F. the space between two nonparallel rays that share an endpoint

G. lines that cross at only one point

H. a line with two endpoints

I. lines that never intersect

DAY 12

Read the story. Then, answer the questions.

Tara found a pair of pink sunglasses on the bus. They had red lightning bolts on the earpieces. Tara liked them. After lunch, she put on the sunglasses to wear at recess. A girl ran to her and said, "Excuse me, but I think those are mine." Tara's heart sank.

20.   What do you think Tara will do? _____

_____

21.   Which clues helped you decide? _____

_____

Read each clue. Then, write the missing vowels to complete each word.

22.	a sea animal with eight legs	____ct____p____s
23.	a reptile that lives in a swamp	cr____c____d____l____
24.	a very small house	c____tt____g____
25.	something to keep the rain off	____mbr____ll____
26.	something that is completely different	____pp____s____t____
27.	a place that has little rain	d____s____rt

FITNESS FLASH: Do five push-ups.

* See page ii.

PLACE STICKER HERE

Write *right*, *straight*, *acute*, or *obtuse* to identify each angle.

EXAMPLES:

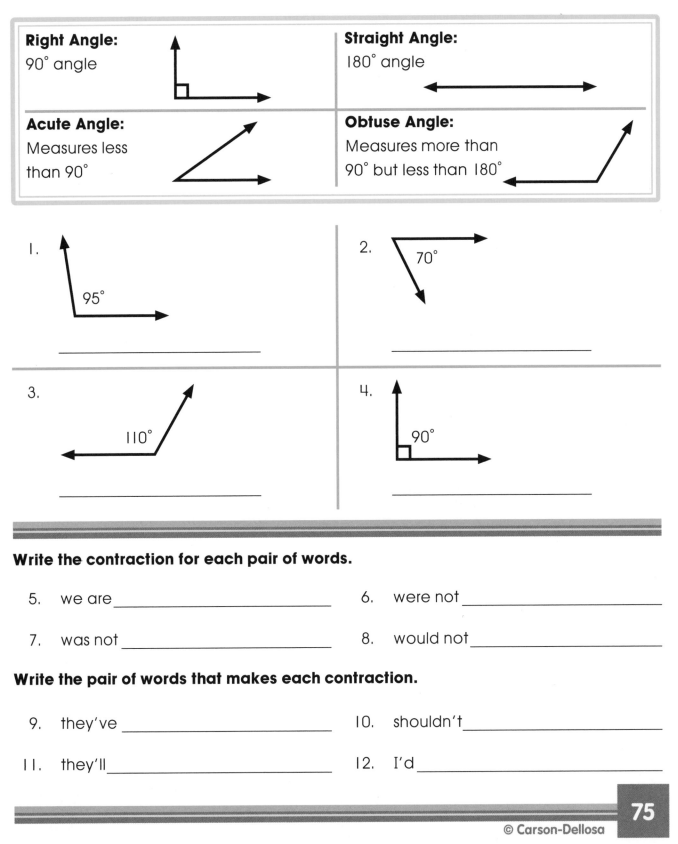

Right Angle:
90° angle

Straight Angle:
180° angle

Acute Angle:
Measures less
than 90°

Obtuse Angle:
Measures more than
90° but less than 180°

1. 95°

    _____

2. 70°

    _____

3. 110°

    _____

4. 90°

    _____

Write the contraction for each pair of words.

5. we are _____

6. were not _____

7. was not _____

8. would not _____

Write the pair of words that makes each contraction.

9. they've _____

10. shouldn't _____

11. they'll _____

12. I'd _____

DAY 13

Read the directions from the oatmeal box. Then, answer the questions.

> ### Instant Oatmeal
> 1. Empty the package into a microwave-safe bowl.
> 2. Add ⅔ cup (156 mL) water and stir.
> 3. Microwave on high for 1 to 2 minutes; stir.
> 4. Pour some milk on top if desired.
> 5. Let cool; eat with a spoon.

13. What do the directions tell you how to make?

    A. oatmeal   B. instant oatmeal   C. cold cereal

14. What is the first step? _____

15. What materials do you need? _____

    _____

16. How long should it take to make this?

    A. a few seconds   B. a few minutes   C. 30 minutes

Write the prefix _re-_ or _un-_ in each blank to complete the sentences.

17. Please _____move your shoes before you come in.

18. That was an _____usual movie.

19. I would like to _____new the magazine subscription.

20. That was an _____common rainstorm.

21. You will have to _____tell the story later.

> **FACTOID:** Angel Falls in Venezuela is the tallest waterfall on Earth at 3,212 feet (979 meters).

PLACE STICKER HERE

Subtract to find each difference.

1.	300 − 130	2.	510 − 250	3.	804 − 163	4.	905 − 662	5.	404 − 142

6.	623 − 257	7.	771 − 704	8.	900 − 156	9.	435 − 297	10.	500 − 297

Write a sentence for each word in the word bank.

hooves	lives	leaves	scarves	shelves

11. _____

_____

12. _____

_____

13. _____

_____

14. _____

_____

15. _____

_____

DAY 14

Study the table of contents. Then, answer the questions.

16. What chapter should you read to learn about writing a story?

    _____

17. On what page should you start reading to learn about commas?

    _____

18. On what page should you start reading to learn how to describe what something looks like?_____

Table of Contents

Communicating with Others 9
Writing a Story 16
Word Meanings 20
Following Directions 25
Using Words Correctly 32
Commas 40
Proofreading 53
Describing Words 57

Write the correct word from the word bank on each line to complete the story.

| classroom | backpack | breakfast | playground | homework |

My School Day

My stepfather wakes me up to get dressed and eat _____ .

I pack my _____ and go to school. I work at my desk in the

_____ . At recess, my friends and I go to the

_____ . At the end

of the day, our teacher writes our _____ assignment on the board.

FITNESS FLASH: Do 10 lunges.

* See page ii.

PLACE STICKER HERE

Solve each word problem. Show your work.

1. Thad planted 5 seeds in each of 9 holes. How many seeds did he plant?

2. Mia has the same number of nickels as she has dimes. She has $1.80 worth of dimes. How many nickels does she have?

3. Jill babysat 4 times last week. She made $4 one night, $5.25 on two different nights, and $6.40 on another night. How much did Jill make altogether?

4. There were 95 children on the bus. Then, 12 got off at the first stop. Twenty-two got off at the second stop. How many children were left on the bus?

Write an ending to the story.

The three friends had not seen Logan for a long time. They were standing in the main room of the natural history museum. "He was here a little while ago," said Kim. The museum was closing. Most of the other visitors had already left.

"Logan likes the dinosaur exhibit and the astronomy room," said Craig. "Maybe we should go look there."

Just then, a museum guard said, "Sorry, but the museum is closing. You'll have to come back tomorrow."

_____

_____

_____

_____

DAY 15

Answer each question about the coordinate grid.

5. Which fruit is located at (3,4)?

   _____

6. Circle the fruit located at (2,2).

7. Draw a peach at (5,3).

8. Which fruit is located at (5,5)?

   _____

9. At which coordinate is the pear located?

   _____

10. Draw a square around the fruit located at (4,2).

A simile compares two unlike things using the words *like* or *as*. Complete each sentence by making a comparison.

EXAMPLE: The daffodils were as yellow as _lemons_.

11. The piano keys were as white as _____.

12. The fireworks were as bright as the _____.

13. His eyes were as green as the _____.

14. The balloons were like a bunch of _____.

15. Her eyes sparkled like _____.

16. The wind was as gentle as _____.

CHARACTER CHECK: Why is it important to be someone people can trust? Write your answer on a separate sheet of paper.

PLACE STICKER HERE

Write the total for each group of money.

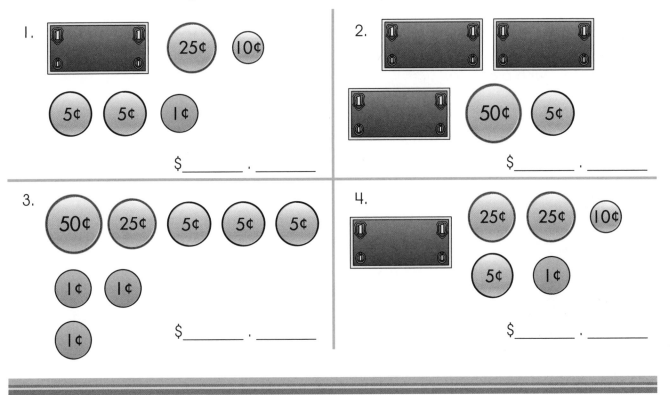

1.

25¢   10¢

5¢   5¢   1¢

$_____ . _____

2.

50¢   5¢

$_____ . _____

3.

50¢   25¢   5¢   5¢   5¢

1¢   1¢

1¢

$_____ . _____

4.

25¢   25¢   10¢

5¢   1¢

$_____ . _____

The main idea tells what a story is about. Underline the sentence in each story that tells the main idea.

5.   Penny's dog Coco likes to eat special snacks. Coco eats carrots. She also likes cheese. Her favorite snack is peanut butter dog biscuits. Penny makes sure that Coco does not eat too many snacks. They also go for a walk every afternoon.

6.   Oliver Owl is teaching Owen Owl to fly. Oliver tells Owen to perch on the highest branch of the tallest tree. "Then, jump and flap your wings as hard as you can," he says. Owen is nervous, but he trusts Oliver. He jumps from the branch and flaps his wings. Oliver cheers as Owen starts to fly! Later, Owen says that Oliver is good at teaching little owls how to fly.

Difficult Decisions

Self-discipline means making yourself do what you know you should. Showing self-discipline can be difficult. But, it becomes easier with practice.

Read the following situation. On a separate sheet of paper, write the possible consequence of not using self-discipline. Then, write the reward for showing self-discipline.

You have been learning to play guitar, and you have become pretty good. During the school year, you practiced for at least 20 minutes every day. Your lessons start again in August. Sometimes, other activities pop up during the summer, like swimming practice and other fun outdoor activities. Playing guitar every day can seem like a chore when there are other cool things to do.

What is the funniest thing your grandparents or other relatives have told you about another family member? Retell the story.

_____

_____

_____

_____

_____

FACTOID: Baby blue whales can gain up to nine pounds (4.1 kg) per hour, or more than 200 pounds (90.7 kg) per day.

PLACE STICKER HERE

Write the correct unit of measurement to complete each sentence.

I meter (m) = 100 centimeters (cm)	I kilometer (km) = 1,000 meters (m)

1. Reid is 150 _____ tall.

2. Paige's room is 5 _____ wide.

3. Whitney's hand is 14 _____ long and 5 _____ wide.

4. Mr. Suarez drove his car 84 _____ the first hour.

5. The distance from Chicago, Illinois, to Denver, Colorado, is 1,466 _____ .

6. Myla's kitchen is approximately 7 _____ wide.

7. The flagpole at the post office is 46 _____ tall.

8. Lin and Tara walked approximately 3 _____ in 30 minutes.

A pronoun is a word that takes the place of a noun. Read each sentence. Then, circle the noun(s) that each underlined pronoun is replacing.

EXAMPLE:

Betty has a (computer.) She keeps <u>it</u> on her desk.

9. Liv forgot her umbrella. She went home to get <u>it</u>.

10. Benji asked Juan if <u>he</u> was going to play baseball this year.

11. Amira and Becca both collect seashells. Sometimes, <u>they</u> trade with each other.

12. Rachel plays the violin, and sometimes <u>she</u> sings too.

13. We gave our dog a new toy. Fido barked when he saw <u>it</u>.

14. Our school bus is always crowded, and <u>it</u> is usually noisy too.

DAY 17

Find the area of each figure.

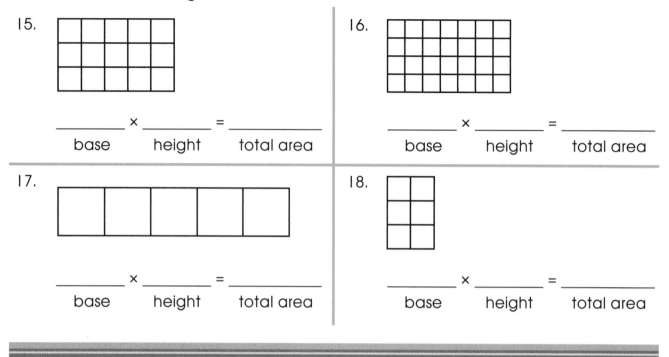

15.

_____ × _____ = _____
base   height   total area

16.

_____ × _____ = _____
base   height   total area

17.

_____ × _____ = _____
base   height   total area

18.

_____ × _____ = _____
base   height   total area

Read the story. Then, answer the questions.

The children were playing baseball in the empty lot. Brooke was at bat. She swung hard and hit the ball farther than anyone else that day. The ball sailed across the lot and smashed through Ms. Havel's window. Brooke knew that Ms. Havel would be upset. The other children scattered and ran for home. Brooke looked at the broken window. Then, she started walking toward the house.

19. What do you think Brooke will do? _____

_____

20. Which clues helped you decide? _____

_____

FITNESS FLASH: Do 10 sit-ups.

* See page ii.

PLACE STICKER HERE

Write the missing factors.

1. _____ × 3 = 6

2. _____ × 6 = 30

3. 4 × _____ = 16

4. 3 × _____ = 18

5. 7 × _____ = 14

6. _____ × 9 = 18

7. _____ × 5 = 5

8. 12 × _____ = 12

9. _____ × 8 = 24

10. 1 × _____ = 9

11. 4 × _____ = 28

12. 9 × _____ = 81

13. 3 × _____ = 21

14. _____ × 5 = 25

15. _____ × 7 = 49

16. _____ × 2 = 4

17. 4 × _____ = 24

18. _____ × 8 = 64

Read each group of related words. Write two more related words for each group.

EXAMPLE:

robin, owl, pigeon _____quail_____ _____pheasant_____

19. peaches, apples, pears _____ _____

20. spoon, bowl, cup _____ _____

21. lake, pond, river _____ _____

22. branches, sticks, wood _____ _____

23. lemonade, water, milk _____ _____

24. dollar, dime, penny _____ _____

25. carrot, celery, cucumber _____ _____

26. dress, shoes, skirt _____ _____

27. tennis, golf, racquetball _____ _____

DAY 18

Write the correct word from the word bank on each line to complete the passage.

plant	heat	sunlight	Earth	oxygen	plants

Sunlight is very important to our planet, _____.

Most of our food comes from _____ life.

_____ also give off the _____ we breathe. Without

_____, plants would die, and we would not have

food or air. The _____ of the sun also warms Earth.

Without it, we would freeze.

Write a synonym from the word bank for each word.

alter	error	connect	afraid	jewel
~~simple~~	cent	present	finish	sofa

EXAMPLE:

easy _____*simple*_____

29. change_____

31. scared_____

33. gift _____

35. complete_____

28. penny_____

30. mistake_____

32. couch_____

34. join_____

36. gem_____

FACTOID: It took American pioneers from four to six months to travel the 2,000-mile (3,200-kilometer) Oregon Trail.

PLACE STICKER HERE

Solve each problem.

1. 2)24   2.   6   3. 3)63   4. 3)99   5.   46
              × 7   − 28

6.   38   7.   83   8.   57   9.   8   10.   4
    + 17   − 47   + 34   × 4   × 7

11. 2)64   12. 7)70   13.   804   14.   132   15.   176
                          − 238   − 78   + 394

Write the correct compound word from the word bank on each line to complete the story.

nighttime	backyard	butterfly
outside	doghouse	weekends

I like the _____ because I get to spend time

_____ with my dog Rusty. In the morning, Rusty

comes out of his _____ to play. We play in the

_____ . Rusty likes to bark at the _____ that lives in the garden.

When _____ comes, Rusty and I are ready to sleep!

DAY 19

Draw lines to divide each shape according to the fraction given.

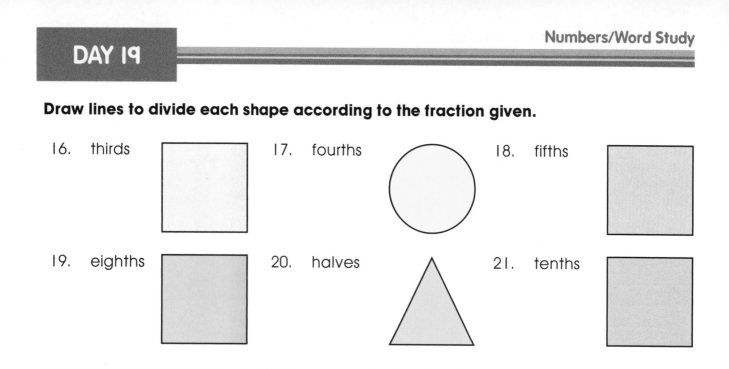

16. thirds

17. fourths

18. fifths

19. eighths

20. halves

21. tenths

Write each word from the word bank under the correct heading.

buttermilk	snowstorm	replanted	peaceful	daylight
airplane	selection	sleepless	football	unpacked

Compound Words

_____

_____

_____

_____

_____

Words with Prefixes or Suffixes

_____

_____

_____

_____

_____

FITNESS FLASH: Do 10 squats.

* See page ii.

PLACE STICKER HERE

88

Read the passage. Then, answer the questions.

Flash Floods

Rain is good for people and plants. When it rains too much, though, people could be in danger. A flash flood occurs when a lot of rain falls quickly, filling the streets faster than the water can drain. Driving is very dangerous in a flash flood. A person's car could be swept away. If you live in an area where flash flooding is likely, you should listen to radio or TV news reports when it starts to rain. Be ready to leave your home with your family if a newscaster says to move to higher ground. If you leave on foot, do not walk through moving water. Your parents should not drive through standing water unless it is less than 6 inches (15.24 cm) deep. After a flood, listen to news reports. A newscaster will tell you when you can return home safely and when the water from your tap will be safe to drink.

1. What is the main idea of this passage?
   A. Flash floods can be dangerous and occur suddenly.
   B. Never drive through a flooded area.
   C. Take important items with you when you leave your home.

2. What happens during a flash flood? _____

   _____

3. What could happen to a car in a flash flood? _____

   _____

4. What should you do when it starts to rain? _____

   _____

5. When should you leave your home? _____

   _____

6. What should you do after a flood? _____

   _____

DAY 20

Write the time for each clock.

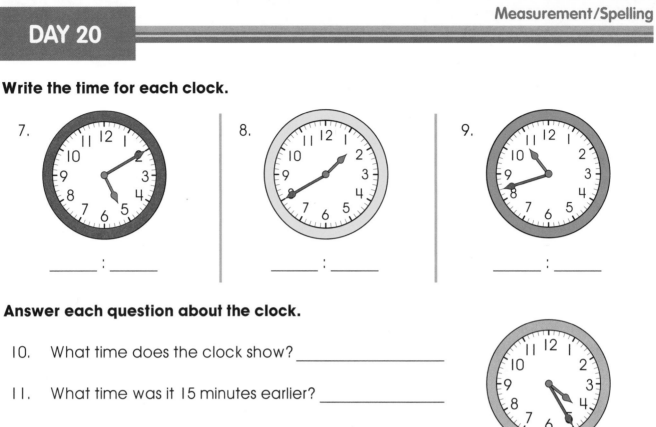

7. _____ : _____

8. _____ : _____

9. _____ : _____

Answer each question about the clock.

10. What time does the clock show? _____

11. What time was it 15 minutes earlier? _____

12. What time will it be in half an hour? _____

13. What time would the clock show if you switched the hands? _____

Circle each correctly spelled word. Then, write it in the blank to complete each sentence.

14. Astronauts are_____ while they are in space.

   waitless   weightless   waghtless   wateless

15. The _____children helped their mother rake leaves.

   thotful   toughtful   thoughtful   thowghtful

16. You need to remember to keep your doctor's _____ .

   apointment   apowntment   appointment

CHARACTER CHECK: What is the golden rule? On a separate sheet of paper, explain the rule using your own words.

PLACE STICKER HERE

Bounce Away!

How much height does a ball lose with each bounce?

Energy is the ability to do work. Potential energy is the energy that an object has because of its position. The energy of an object in motion is called kinetic energy. If you hold a tennis ball above the ground, it has potential energy due to its position. When the ball is released, gravity pulls it down. The ball's potential energy becomes kinetic energy.

Materials:
* meterstick
* tennis ball

Procedure:
Hold the meterstick vertically with one end against the floor. Hold the tennis ball so that the bottom is at the zero mark.

Drop the ball from a height of 1 meter. Watch carefully to determine the height of the first, second, and third bounces. Round the answer to the nearest centimeter and record the information on the table below.

Because of the speed at which the ball bounces, you may want to ask another person to help you measure the height of the ball's bounces.

Bounce	Height of Bounce
1	
2	
3	

What's This All About?
The shape of the tennis ball changes slightly when it hits the floor. Some energy is lost as heat (due to friction from air resistance) and when the ball changes shape. Because of the lost energy, the ball will not bounce to the same height it was dropped from. After the ball hits the ground, it returns to its original shape. The energy becomes upward motion as the ball bounces into the air.

BONUS

Separating Salt and Pepper

How can a mixture of salt and pepper be separated?

Some mixtures are homogenous. This means that they combine evenly. For example, when you mix sugar and water you get sugar water. The sugar spreads evenly throughout the water.

If you mix sand and water you get a heterogeneous mixture. The sand sinks to the bottom and will not stay mixed with the water.

In this experiment, determine whether salt and pepper is a homogenous or heterogeneous mixture.

Materials:

- balance or kitchen scale
- pepper
- tray
- balloon
- salt
- your hair (clean and dry)

Procedure:

Use the balance or scale to weigh several teaspoons of salt and pepper. Then, mix the salt and pepper on the tray. Gently shake the tray so that the mixture forms a single layer. Then, blow up the balloon.

Keep your hand in the same place on the balloon and rub the other side of the balloon back and forth about 20 times on your clean, dry hair. Then, hold the balloon about 1 inch (2.5 cm) above the mixture of salt and pepper. The salt will be attracted to the balloon. Most of the pepper will stay where it is.

Brush the salt off the balloon and onto the balance or scale. Measure the salt again to find its mass. Record your data on the table.

Trial	Amount of Salt Placed in Mixture	Amount of Salt Removed from Mixture
1		
2		
3		

Is the mixture of salt and pepper homogeneous or heterogeneous? _____

* See page ii.

Lines of Latitude

Lines of latitude are imaginary lines that run east to west on a map. They are marked in degrees (°) and help people locate places around the world. The equator is the line at 0° latitude. The lines of latitude on the map below are measured in 20° segments from the equator. Places north of the equator have the letter *N* after their degrees. Places south of the equator have the letter *S* after their degrees.

Study the map. Then, answer the questions.

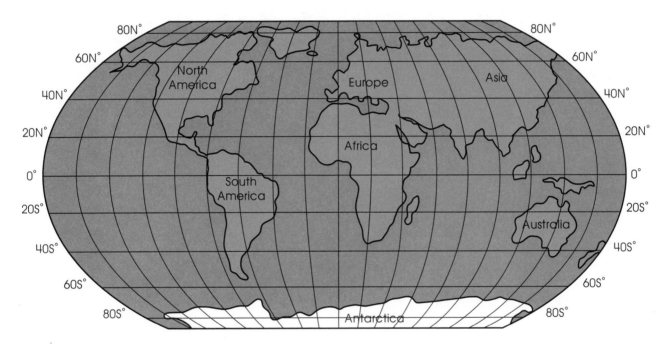

1. The equator is at _____ ° latitude.

2. For locations in North America, the latitude should be followed by the letter____ .

3. The latitude for the southern tip of South America would be followed by the letter_____ .

4. Use a red crayon or marker to trace the equator.

BONUS

Latitude and Longitude

Use the map to find the cities located at each latitude and longitude. Then, write the name of each city.

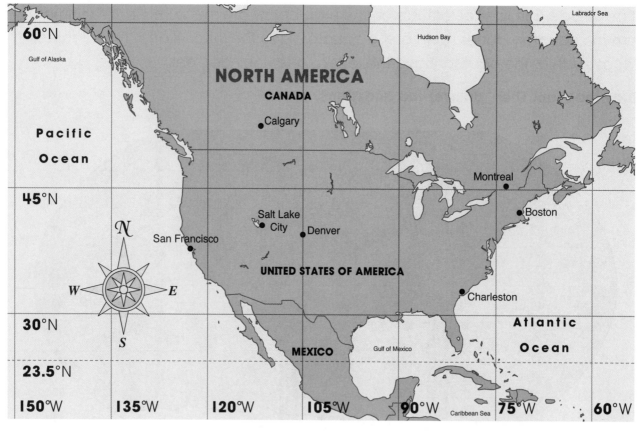

	Latitude	Longitude	City
1.	51°N	114°W	_____
2.	39°N	105°W	_____
3.	42°N	71°W	_____
4.	32°N	79°W	_____
5.	45°N	73°W	_____
6.	40°N	111°W	_____
7.	37°N	122°W	_____

Coat of Arms

A coat of arms is a design that belongs to a particular person or family. The colors, symbols, and backgrounds used in a coat of arms all have special meanings and say something about the coat of arms's owner. For example, the color blue may represent truth and loyalty, while a lion may represent courage.

Create a coat of arms. Think of some qualities that you have and are proud of. Brainstorm ways that you could represent those qualities on your coat of arms. Go online with an adult if you need more information. Then, draw your coat of arms in the box.

BONUS

Take It Outside!

Take a tape measure outside four times throughout one day. Each time, have an adult measure the length of your shadow and record the measurements. Then, with an adult, use the computer to search for information about Earth's rotation around the sun. This will help explain why the length of your shadow changes throughout the day.

With an adult, take a thesaurus, a notebook, and a pencil outside. Find a safe, comfortable spot to sit and write the things you see, such as a bird flying, a bee flying, or an airplane flying. Then, find some of the overused words you wrote, such as *flying*. Use a thesaurus to find replacement words that provide better descriptions, such as *soaring*, *gliding*, or *hovering*. Use these new words whenever you can.

How do you find how tall a tree is without a long measuring tape and a tall ladder? You can use the measurements of a tree's shadow and the shadow of a 12-inch ruler to find the height of a tree. First, go outside with an adult and measure the length of a tree's shadow with a measuring tape, yardstick, or meterstick. Then, stand the ruler on its end at a 90° angle from the ground. Use the measuring tape, a yardstick, or a meterstick to find the length of the ruler's shadow. Record the length of each shadow and convert the measurements to the same unit, such as inches. To find the height of the tree, divide the length of the tree's shadow by the length of the ruler's shadow. Then, multiply the answer by the length of the ruler.

For example, if the answer is 10, this means that the tree's shadow is 10 times longer than the ruler, which makes the tree about 10 feet tall.

* See page ii.

Monthly Goals

Think of three goals to set for yourself this month. For example, you may want to exercise for 20 minutes each day. Write your goals on the lines and review them with an adult.

Place a sticker next to each goal that you complete. Feel proud that you have met your goals!

1. _____
   PLACE STICKER HERE

2. _____
   PLACE STICKER HERE

3. _____
   PLACE STICKER HERE

Word List

The following words are used in this section. They are good words for you to know. Read each word. Use a dictionary to look up each word that you do not know. Then, write two sentences. Use a word from the word list in each sentence.

central	murmuring
compass	organized
discuss	rural
interviewing	urban
magnet	vapor

1. _____

_____

2. _____

_____

Introduction to Endurance

Physical Endurance

What do playing tag, jumping rope, and riding your bike have in common? They are all great ways to build endurance!

Having endurance means doing an activity for a long time before your body becomes tired. Your heart is stronger when you have endurance. Your muscles receive more oxygen.

Use the warm summer mornings and sunny days to go outside. Pick activities that you enjoy. Invite a family member on a walk or a bike ride. Play a game of basketball with friends. Leave the less active times for when it is dark, too hot, or raining.

Set an endurance goal this summer. For example, you might jump rope every day until you can jump for two minutes without stopping. Set new goals when you meet your old ones. Be proud of your endurance success!

Endurance and Character Development

Showing mental endurance means sticking with something. You can show mental endurance every day. Staying with a task when you might want to quit and keeping at it until it is done are ways that you can show mental endurance.

Build your mental endurance this summer. Think of a time when you were frustrated or bored. Maybe you wanted to take swimming lessons. But, after a few early morning lessons, it was not as fun as you imagined. Think about some key points, such as how you asked all spring to take lessons. Be positive. Remind yourself that you have taken only a few lessons. You might get used to the early morning practices. Think of ways to make the lessons more enjoyable, such as sleeping a few extra minutes during the morning car ride. Quitting should be the last option.

Build your mental endurance now. It will help prepare you for challenges you may face later!

Study the pictograph. Then, answer each question.

Month	Tires Sold
Jan.	O O O O O C
Feb.	O O
March	O C
April	O O O C
May	O

Key
O = 500 tires

1. How many more tires were sold in April than in February?

   _____

2. What is the difference between the least number of tires sold in a month and the greatest number of tires sold in a month?

   _____

Read the paragraph. Then, answer the questions.

Sandra's mother offered to help her get ready for the new school year. Sandra grew a full inch taller over the summer. Her shoes were too tight, and her pants were almost above her ankles.

3. What do you think Sandra and her mother will do? _____

   _____

   _____

4. Which clues helped you decide? _____

   _____

   _____

DAY 1

Complete the table.

	Total Price	Amount Given to Clerk	Change Received
EXAMPLE:	$1.35	$1.50	$0.15
5.	$2.50	$5.00	
6.	$0.95	$1.00	
7.	$1.80	$2.00	
8.	$6.42	$10.00	
9.	$9.35	$20.00	
10.	$5.55	$6.00	
11.	$13.95	$20.00	
12.	$85.00	$100.00	

Write the base word of each word.

13. playful _____

14. disinterest _____

15. rewrite _____

16. uncover _____

17. spoonful _____

18. quickly _____

19. happiness _____

20. doubtful _____

21. kindness _____

22. recover _____

FACTOID: No two snowflakes are exactly alike.

PLACE STICKER HERE

Read the passage. Then, answer the questions.

Food Webs

A food web is a drawing that shows how different living things are connected. In a food web, the living things at the bottom are eaten by the animals directly above them. For example, a food web might start at the bottom with plants. Plants do not eat other living things. Above these plants might be small animals, such as mice, that eat plants. Larger animals, such as owls and snakes, eat mice. A food web can tell us what might happen if certain plants or animals disappear from an **ecosystem**, or the surroundings in which all of the plants and animals live. In the food web described above, if something happened to the plants, then the mice would not have as much food. This would affect the owls and snakes, who would also not have enough food. Soon, there would be fewer of each type of animal. This is why it is important to protect all living things in an ecosystem, not just the larger ones.

1. What is the main idea of this passage?
    A. Food webs show how all living things are connected.
    B. Owls and snakes are the most important animals.
    C. Only the animals at the top of the food web should be protected.

2. What is a food web? _____

    _____

3. What might happen if the plants in a food web disappear? _____

    _____

4. What is an ecosystem?
    A. a food web for very large animals
    B. the surroundings where a group of plants and animals live
    C. a place where only plants grow

5. Why is it important to protect all living things in an ecosystem? _____

    _____

DAY 2

Find each equivalent measurement.

2 cups = 1 pint	4 quarts = 1 gallon
2 pints = 1 quart	16 cups = 1 gallon

6. 5 quarts = _____ pints

7. 3 gallons = _____ pints

8. 4 cups = _____ pints

9. 2 pints = _____ cups

10. _____ gallons = 16 pints

11. 5 gallons = _____ quarts

12. _____ pints = 2 quarts

13. 3 quarts = _____ cups

Double the Fun (and Falls)

Boost your endurance and help a friend or family member get fit too. Make an outdoor obstacle course using soft objects, such as piles of leaves, to run around and hop over. Mark a turnaround spot so that you can retrace your hops and repeat the course. Use two strong, soft pieces of fabric to tie yourself to your partner above the ankles and knees. Remember that you must work together to complete this course. For the first time through, walk the route and discuss your strategy. For the following turn, time your performance. Then, set a goal and repeat the course to try to beat your time. Encourage each other to challenge yourselves. Keep going until you reach your goal!

FITNESS FLASH: Jog in place for 30 seconds.

* See page ii.

PLACE STICKER HERE

Complete each fact family.

1. 5 × 3 = _____

    _____ × _____ = _____

    _____ ÷ _____ = _____

    _____ ÷ _____ = _____

2. 21 ÷ 3 = _____

    _____ ÷ _____ = _____

    _____ × _____ = _____

    _____ × _____ = _____

3. 30 ÷ 6 = _____

    _____ ÷ _____ = _____

    _____ × _____ = _____

    _____ × _____ = _____

Find each probability.

Chloe has 11 pencils in her pencil box. Two pencils are orange, 3 pencils are blue, 5 pencils are yellow, and 1 pencil is green.

4. What is the probability that Chloe will pull out a black pencil?

    _____

5. What is the probability that Chloe will pull out an orange pencil?

    _____

6. What is the probability that Chloe will pull out a green pencil?

    _____

7. What is the probability that Chloe will pull out a blue pencil?

    _____

8. What is the probability that Chloe will pull out a yellow pencil?

    _____

9. What color pencil is Chloe most likely to pull out of her pencil box?

    _____

Read the passage. Then, answer the questions.

Edward Murrow

Edward Murrow was an American journalist. He became famous during World War II. Murrow was born in 1908 in North Carolina. After college, he began working for a radio station. Many Americans listened to his live broadcasts during the bombing of London, England, in September 1939. Before Murrow's reports, people in the United States learned about the war through newsreels in movie theaters or articles in newspapers. Now, they could learn about the war in London as it was happening. After the war, Murrow worked as a reporter in radio, then in television. He became known for interviewing, or asking questions of, important people. Other newscasters followed in Murrow's footsteps. Today, we still rely on reporters in other countries for news and information. And, we still listen to reporters' conversations with famous people.

10. What is the main idea of this passage?
   A. Edward Murrow was a brave American journalist.
   B. Edward Murrow talked to many famous people.
   C. Edward Murrow worked in London.

11. What type of company did Murrow work for after college?

   _____

12. How did people learn about the war before Murrow's reports?

   _____

13. What did Murrow do after the war ended? _____

   _____

14. How did Murrow change the way journalists work? _____

   _____

FACTOID: Giant squids have the largest eyes of any creature on Earth.

PLACE STICKER HERE

Study the bar graph. Then, answer each question.

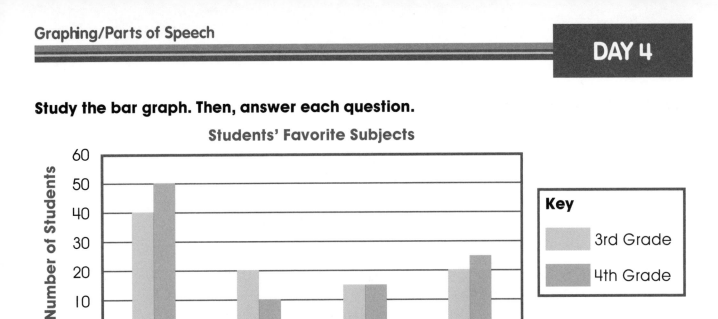

1. What is the total number of students who like social studies?

   _____

2. How many total students are in 3rd grade? Fourth grade?

   _____

3. Which subject has the greatest difference between 3rd and 4th grade?

   _____

4. How many more students like math than reading in 3rd grade? Fourth grade?

   _____

Circle the adverb in each sentence. Then, underline the verb each adverb modifies.

5. The dogs barked loudly at the sound of the doorbell.

6. I looked everywhere for my coat.

7. Nancy swims faster than I do.

8. Greg walked slowly up the driveway.

9. Valerie awoke early on Saturday morning.

10. Let's play outside in the front yard.

DAY 4

Divide to find each quotient.

11. 3)18   12. 4)24   13. 3)21   14. 4)36   15. 8)32

16. 5)40   17. 6)36   18. 9)36   19. 8)40   20. 9)27

Add commas where they belong in each phrase or sentence.

21.   My family visits Spring Grove Minnesota every year in the summer.

22.   Dear Grandpa

23.   Yours truly

24.   On October 9 2009 Carolyn saw the play.

25.   My aunt and uncle live in North Branch New York.

26.   Dear Jon

27.   January 1 2010

28.   Paris Texas is located in the northeastern part of the state.

FITNESS FLASH: Hop on your right foot for 30 seconds.

* See page ii.

PLACE STICKER HERE

Read the story. Then, answer the questions.

Ivy's grandmother will celebrate her 70th birthday soon. Ivy wants to get her grandmother a special gift, but she spent her money on new books instead. Ivy loves reading about Mexico. Her grandmother came from Mexico, and she read to Ivy when Ivy was little. Lately, her grandmother's eyesight has been failing, so she can no longer see the words on the page.

1. What do you think Ivy will do? _____

    _____

2. Which clues helped you decide? _____

    _____

Complete each sentence with the correct word from the parentheses.

3. The baseball game went _____ for the Spartans right from the first inning. (well, better, best)

4. The first batter, Monroe, always hits _____ . (well, better, best)

5. Monroe runs the bases _____ than most players on his team. (well, better, best)

6. Stanley, the second batter, usually hits even _____ than Monroe. (well, better, best)

7. The pitcher threw his _____ pitches to Stanley. (well, better, best)

8. Stanley hit the ball _____ , and it flew over the fence for a two-run home run. (well, better, best)

9. Things went _____ for the Tigers in the second half of the game than in the first. (badly, worse, worst)

DAY 5

Solve each word problem. Show your work.

10. Bobbi made 8 quarts of punch for the party. How many cups did she make?

11. Two boxes of gold weigh 4 pounds 8 ounces. Each pound costs $400. How much are the boxes worth in all?

12. Ms. Lackey gave each student in her class a calculator. Each calculator weighed 16 ounces. If Ms. Lackey gave each of her 20 students a calculator, how many pounds did the calculators weigh in all?

13. Virginia's school ordered 20 boxes of milk. In each box, there were 35 containers of milk. By the end of the week, 265 containers were used. How many containers were left?

Fit Tag

Get fit with this version of freeze tag! Invite several friends or family members to play. Start by choosing someone to be "it." That person must chase and tag everyone until all of the players are "frozen." Frozen players perform an ongoing exercise, such as jumping jacks or running in place. Players who are free can unfreeze their teammates by tapping them on their shoulders. The last person frozen becomes "it." Continue playing until everyone has gotten a good endurance-boosting workout.

CHARACTER CHECK: "When you get to the end of your rope, tie a knot and hang on." Franklin D. Roosevelt

* See page ii.

Read the story. Then, write the meaning of each word.

Gabe lives in a large city with his grandparents. The building that he and his grandparents live in is very tall and has different sets of rooms for each family that lives there. This building is called an apartment building. In this community, all of the buildings are close together. People do not have to go far to get things they need in this urban area. Gabe's cousin, Jasper, lives in a rural, or country, community. He plays in his large backyard instead of a park like Gabe. There is a lot of space between houses where Jasper lives. Both Gabe's and Jasper's neighborhoods have schools, hospitals, and stores.

1. community _____

_____

2. urban _____

_____

3. rural _____

_____

Use the word bank to label each part of the friendly letter.

body
closing
greeting
signature
heading

_____ { 1921 King Street
Boise, Idaho 83704
August 2, 2009

_____ Dear Sara,

_____ { I am having a great time at camp.
I swim every day and hike a lot too.
Yesterday, our group hiked five miles.
I hope you are feeling better.

_____ Your friend,

_____ Fiona

DAY 6

Read the passage. Then, answer the questions.

Early Computers

Have you ever used a computer at school, at the library, or at home? Today, a computer can fit on a desktop or in your lap. A computer of the past took up a whole room! One of the first computers was called the ENIAC, which stood for Electronic Numerical Integrator and Calculator. It took up 1,800 square feet (about 167 sq. m), weighed nearly 50 tons, and cost $500,000. The ENIAC took three years to build and was designed for the U.S. Army. It required a team of six people to **program** it, or tell it what to do. The ENIAC was used from 1947 to 1955. In contrast, a personal computer today can weigh less than 2 pounds (about 1 kg) and can be operated by one person at a time.

4. What is the main idea of this passage?
    A.   The ENIAC was an early computer.
    B.   Computers of the past were very different from computers today.
    C.   Students can do their homework on computers.

5. How large was ENIAC? _____

6. What does the word *program* mean in this passage?
    A.   build a computer
    B.   require six people to use
    C.   tell a computer what to do

7. When was the ENIAC used?_____

8. How are computers today different from those in the past?_____

_____

_____

_____

FACTOID: It takes sunlight just over eight minutes to reach Earth.

PLACE
STICKER
HERE

Write the number of sides and vertices for each polygon.

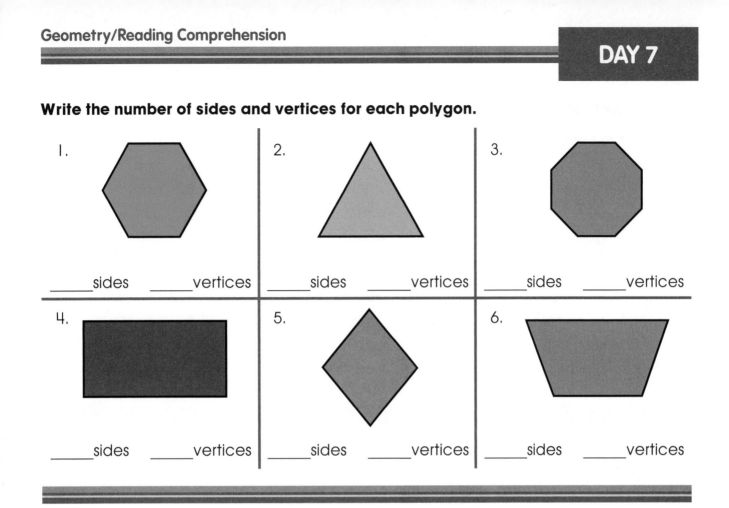

1. _____ sides _____ vertices

2. _____ sides _____ vertices

3. _____ sides _____ vertices

4. _____ sides _____ vertices

5. _____ sides _____ vertices

6. _____ sides _____ vertices

In each sentence, underline the cause and circle the effect.

EXAMPLE: The sky became cloudy, then it started to snow.

7. The cold weather caused frost to cover the windows.

8. The falling snowflakes made my cheeks wet and cold.

9. Snow stuck to my mittens because I had made a snowman.

10. The snowman melted from the heat of the sun.

11. I swam so long in the pool that I needed to put on more sunscreen.

12. Cayce missed the bus because she overslept.

13. Because Shay watched a scary movie on TV, she could not fall asleep.

14. The lady was thirsty, so she went to get a glass of water.

DAY 7

Choose the best unit of measurement for each liquid.

15. a bowl of soup
    A. cup
    B. quart
    C. pint
    D. gallon

16. a swimming pool
    A. cup
    B. quart
    C. pint
    D. gallon

17. a pitcher of water
    A. cup
    B. quart
    C. pint
    D. gallon

18. a glass of juice
    A. milliliter
    B. centiliter
    C. liter
    D. kiloliter

19. water in a bathtub
    A. milliliter
    B. centiliter
    C. liter
    D. kiloliter

20. motor oil
    A. milliliter
    B. centiliter
    C. liter
    D. kiloliter

Circle the pronouns in each sentence.

21. I told her about Janelle's horse.

22. This piece of cake is for him.

23. Liz invited Garrett and me to the party.

24. The table is set for us.

25. We are too late to see the first show.

26. They will be happy to come with us.

27. Clams and turtles have shells. They are protected by them.

FITNESS FLASH: Hop on your right foot for 30 seconds.

* See page ii.

PLACE STICKER HERE

Read the passage. Then, answer the questions.

Planning a City

What do the streets in your city look like? Some cities have streets that are very straight and organized. It is easy to get from one point in the city to another. Other cities have streets that seem to go nowhere. It may be difficult to give directions to your home.

In the past, when a group of people moved to a place and started planning the streets, some of them used something called a grid system. One example of this is found in the city of Philadelphia, Pennsylvania, which is divided into four sections around a central square. The map was laid out by William Penn in 1682. The grid included wide streets that were easy for people to walk down. Penn left London, England, after a fire destroyed most of the city. London had a maze of narrow streets that were hard to move around safely. Penn wanted to make sure that people could get around easily and safely. Many other people followed Penn's ideas when setting up their new cities' street systems.

1. What is the main idea of this passage?
   A. William Penn drew the first grid system.
   B. Planning a city is important for safety and ease of use.
   C. Some streets are straight and organized.

2. What is one good thing about having straight streets? _____

   _____

3. What is a grid system?
   A. a plan for developing a city's streets
   B. an area of the classroom
   C. a TV channel

4. When did Penn leave London? _____

   _____

5. How are Philadelphia's streets different from London's? _____

   _____

DAY 8

A figure is symmetrical if it can be folded in half so that the two parts are congruent. Draw one line of symmetry for each figure.

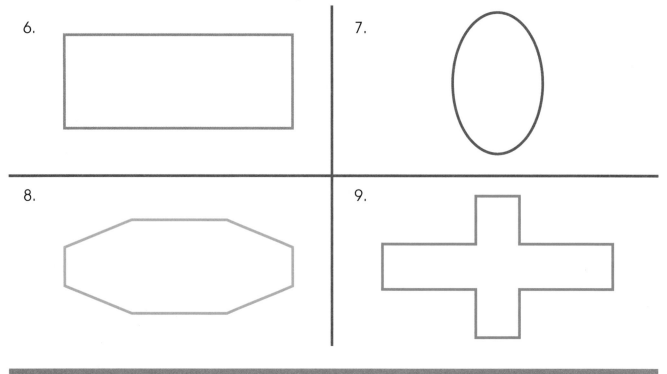

6.

7.

8.

9.

Unscramble the words in parentheses to complete each analogy.

10. Pillows are to soft as boards are to _____ . (rdha)

11. Bells are to ring as car horns are to _____ . (nkho)

12. Hear is to ears as touch is to _____ . (serinfg)

13. Star is to pointed as circle is to _____ . (dunor)

14. Fish is to swim as bird is to _____ . (ylf)

15. Elephant is to large as mouse is to _____ . (malsl)

16. Paint is to brush as draw is to _____ . (cienlp)

FACTOID: A sneeze can travel at a speed of more than 100 miles (160.9 km) per hour.

PLACE STICKER HERE

Use the table to answer each question.

Student Music Lesson Schedule

Day 1 (new students only)	Day 2	Day 3	Day 4	Day 5
Nicole	José	Solina	Greg	Jamie
Naomi	Kira	Jamie	Kipley	Solina
Tanya	Kipley	Greg	Jacob	Rebecca
Michelle	Mark	Rebecca	José	Mark
Fiora	Jacob	Margaret	Kira	Drake

1. Other than Jacob, who has a lesson on day 4? _____

   _____

2. Tanya, Naomi, and Fiora all have a lesson on which day? _____

3. How many lessons is Jacob scheduled for in all? _____

4. Kipley, Naomi, and Mark practice together. Who is the new music student?

   _____

5. How many new students are there altogether? _____

6. Why does Mark not have a lesson on day 1? _____

   _____

If you could be any animal, which animal would you be? Why?

_____

_____

_____

DAY 9

Does the dotted line in each figure represent a line of symmetry? Circle *yes* or *no*.

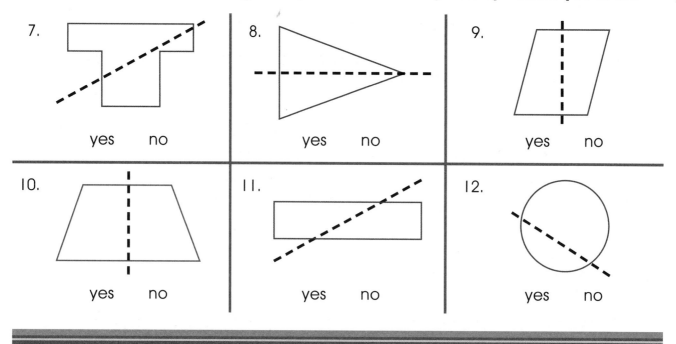

7.

yes   no

8.

yes   no

9.

yes   no

10.

yes   no

11.

yes   no

12.

yes   no

Complete each sentence with the correct form of *good* or *bad* from the parentheses.

13. The weatherperson said that we will have _____ weather on Thursday. (good, better, best)

14. She said that the weather this weekend will be _____ than today. (good, better, best)

15. Sunday will have the _____ weather this week. (good, better, best)

16. Parts of the country are having _____ storms. (bad, worse, worst)

17. The weatherperson is predicting that the _____ of the snow is coming soon. (bad, worse, worst)

18. Florida usually has _____ weather in the winter. (good, better, best)

FITNESS FLASH: Do 10 jumping jacks.

* See page ii.

PLACE STICKER HERE

Read the passage. Then, answer the questions.

Magnets

A magnet is an object with a magnetic field. This means that it pulls things made of iron, steel, or nickel toward it. If you place a paper clip next to a magnet on a table, the paper clip will move toward the magnet. Every magnet has what is called a north pole and a south pole. The north pole of one magnet will stick to the south pole of another magnet. If you try to push the south poles of two magnets together, they will spring apart. Earth has magnetic poles too. Earth is a big magnet! Earth's magnetic poles are not actual places. They are areas of Earth's magnetic field that have a certain property. Although Earth's magnetic poles are different from the poles where polar bears and penguins live, its magnetic poles are near those poles. The north pole of a magnet will always try to point toward Earth's north magnetic pole. A device called a compass works by having a magnetized needle that points toward Earth's magnetic north pole. If you place a compass on a flat surface, the needle should point north.

1. What is the main idea of this passage?
   A. Every magnet has a north pole and a south pole.
   B. Compasses work by pointing to the north.
   C. A magnet is an object with a magnetic field.

2. What happens if you place a paper clip next to a magnet? _____

_____

3. How is Earth like a magnet? _____

4. What happens if you push a north pole and a south pole of two magnets

   together? _____

5. What happens if you push the south poles of two magnets together? _____

_____

6. How does a compass work? _____

DAY 10

Add to find each sum. Write each answer in its simplest form.

7. $\frac{1}{3} + \frac{2}{3} =$

8. $\frac{4}{6} + \frac{5}{6} =$

9. $\frac{1}{6} + \frac{1}{6} =$

10. $\frac{3}{6} + \frac{1}{6} =$

11. $\frac{2}{4} + \frac{2}{4} =$

12. $\frac{1}{2} + \frac{1}{2} =$

13. $\frac{5}{8} + \frac{3}{8} =$

14. $\frac{5}{5} + \frac{2}{5} =$

15. $\frac{2}{10} + \frac{4}{10} =$

A possessive pronoun is a pronoun that shows ownership. Some possessive pronouns include:

mine	ours	your	his	hers	their	its	my	our

Write five sentences in cursive. Use a possessive pronoun in each sentence.

16. _____

17. _____

18. _____

19. _____

20. _____

CHARACTER CHECK: Make a list of five things you are grateful for. Share your list with an adult.

PLACE STICKER HERE

Look at each underlined idiom. Then, choose the correct meaning of each sentence.

1. Cody was <u>back to square one</u> when his dog chewed his science fair project.
   A. Cody stood on a square that was labeled *one*.
   B. Cody had to start his science fair project again from the beginning.
   C. Cody was unhappy that his dog chewed up his science fair project.

2. <u>Time flies</u> when we are having fun.
   A. Time seems to go quickly when we are having fun.
   B. Time has wings and flies like a bird.
   C. Time goes slowly.

3. Torika needs to <u>toe the line</u> if she wants to go to the movies.
   A. Torika needs to behave if she wants to go to the movies.
   B. Torika needs to stand behind a line if she wants to go to the movies.
   C. Torika needs to stand in line for a movie ticket.

The Power of Perseverance

The word *perseverance* means to keep going even if something is difficult. Think of someone you know whom you admire or consider a hero, like a grandparent. Ask this person if you can conduct an interview. Ask your hero questions to try to determine what made him successful. What struggles did he overcome? What made him persevere? Write the answers to those questions. After interviewing your hero, write a key quote from him that explains his perseverance, such as, "I always tried my best because I wanted to be my best." Post the quote where you can see it every day as a reminder to never give up.

DAY 11

Subtract to find each difference. Regroup if needed.

4.	$7.36 − $3.97	5.	$8.90 − $2.49	6.	$7.68 − $4.79

7. $3.85
   − $2.79

8. $7.47
   − $4.58

9. $8.37
   − $2.09

10. $4.76
   − $2.67

11. $6.89
   − $4.78

12. $6.77
   − $2.88

13. $3.76
   − $1.87

What is the best thing you did this summer?

_____

_____

_____

_____

_____

_____

_____

_____

_____

FACTOID: A flea can jump 200 times the length of its body.

PLACE
STICKER
HERE

Write the perimeter of each figure.

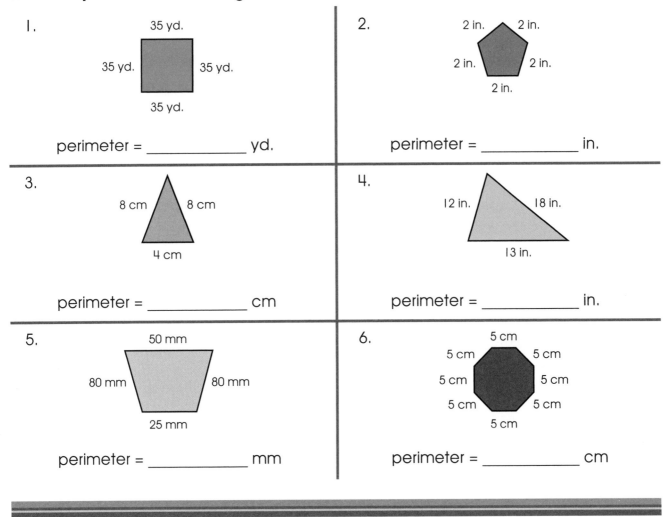

1.

35 yd.

35 yd.   35 yd.

35 yd.

perimeter = _____ yd.

2.

2 in.   2 in.

2 in.   2 in.

2 in.

perimeter = _____ in.

3.

8 cm   8 cm

4 cm

perimeter = _____ cm

4.

12 in.   18 in.

13 in.

perimeter = _____ in.

5.

50 mm

80 mm   80 mm

25 mm

perimeter = _____ mm

6.

5 cm

5 cm   5 cm

5 cm   5 cm

5 cm   5 cm

5 cm

perimeter = _____ cm

Imagine that you are asked to invent a new word. What would the word be, and what would it mean?

_____

_____

_____

_____

_____

DAY 12

Read the passage. Then, answer the questions.

Matter

All matter on Earth exists in one of three states: solid, liquid, or gas. Solids, such as boxes or books, have certain shapes that are difficult to change. Liquids, such as lemonade or orange juice, take the shape of the containers they are in. Gases, such as the air you breathe and helium, spread out to fill the space they are in. It is easy to change water from one state to another. The water you drink is a liquid. When water is heated, such as in a pot on the stove, it becomes a gas. This gas is known as steam, or vapor. Steam can be used in a large machine to make electricity. When water is frozen, such as in a tray in the freezer, it turns to ice. Ice can be used to help a hurt part of the body heal.

7. What is the main idea of this passage?
    A.   Steam is heated water.
    B.   All matter exists as a solid, a liquid, or a gas.
    C.   Ice cubes make water taste better.

8. What are two examples of solids? _____

9. What are two examples of liquids? _____

10. What are two examples of gases? _____

11. Water can exist as a solid, a liquid, or a gas. What is it called in each state?

    _____

12. How are solids, liquids, and gases different from each other? _____

    _____

    _____

    _____

FITNESS FLASH: Jog in place for 30 seconds.

* See page ii.

PLACE STICKER HERE

Add to find each sum. Write each answer in simplest form.

1. $\dfrac{1}{4} + \dfrac{3}{4} =$

2. $\dfrac{3}{5} + \dfrac{2}{5} =$

3. $\dfrac{3}{7} + \dfrac{2}{7} =$

4. $\dfrac{3}{4} + \dfrac{1}{4} =$

5. $\dfrac{1}{7} + \dfrac{1}{7} =$

6. $\dfrac{1}{6} + \dfrac{4}{6} =$

Write the correct homophone from the word bank to complete each sentence.

I	eye	you	ewe	wear	where

7. My friend and _____ ate lunch together.

8. The _____ took care of her lamb.

9. Cory got a speck of dust in his _____ .

10. Do you know _____ to put the books away?

11. Would _____ please hand me that pencil?

12. Hillary will _____ her blue shoes today.

DAY 13

Read each sentence. Write *F* if it is a fact. Write *O* if it is an opinion.

EXAMPLE:

_____**F**_____ Abraham Lincoln was the 16th president of the United States.

13. _____ Spring is the best time of the year.

14. _____ Chocolate cake is the best dessert in the world.

15. _____ Daytime and nighttime depend on the position of the sun in the sky.

16. _____ Dogs are the best pets.

17. _____ Neil Armstrong walked on the moon in 1969.

18. _____ Lava rock was once hot liquid.

19. _____ Eating too much candy is bad for your teeth.

20. _____ Everyone should like chocolate ice cream.

21. _____ Reading is the best way to spend a rainy day.

Describe your dream vacation in detail. Where would you go? What would you do?

_____

_____

_____

_____

_____

FACTOID: A lightning bolt can heat the surrounding air to a temperature of more than 50,000°F (27,760°C).

PLACE STICKER HERE

Read the passage. Then, answer the questions.

Health and Fitness

Health and fitness are important for you and your family. If you start good health habits now, you will have a better chance of being a healthy adult later. You may go to physical education class several times a week, but you should also try to stay fit outside of school. You and your family can make healthy choices together. You can choose fresh fruit for dessert instead of cake. Offer to help make dinner one night, and surprise your family by preparing a delicious salad. You can go for a walk together after dinner instead of watching TV. Exercising can help wake up your brain so that you can do a good job on your homework. Making healthy choices may seem hard now, but it will feel good after a while.

1. What is the main idea of this passage?
   A. Going to physical education class is fun.
   B. Making healthy choices is too hard.
   C. Health and fitness are important for you and your family.

2. What might happen if you start good health habits now? _____

   _____

3. Where should you try to stay fit? _____

   _____

4. What is a better choice than cake for dessert? _____

5. What can you do instead of watching TV after dinner? _____

   _____

6. How does exercise affect your brain? _____

   _____

   _____

DAY 14

Draw a line to match each related division and multiplication problem.

7.	65 ÷ 5	A.	9 × 4
8.	24 ÷ 6	B.	6 × 4
9.	36 ÷ 9	C.	9 × 5
10.	45 ÷ 5	D.	17 × 3
11.	28 ÷ 7	E.	7 × 4
12.	64 ÷ 8	F.	9 × 9
13.	51 ÷ 3	G.	8 × 8
14.	81 ÷ 9	H.	13 × 5

15.	72 ÷ 9	A.	18 × 4
16.	38 ÷ 2	B.	8 × 9
17.	72 ÷ 4	C.	22 × 4
18.	50 ÷ 2	D.	19 × 2
19.	56 ÷ 4	E.	43 × 2
20.	86 ÷ 2	F.	28 × 2
21.	88 ÷ 4	G.	14 × 4
22.	75 ÷ 3	H.	25 × 3

Circle each word that needs a capital letter.

4407 ninth street
hillside, maine 04024

march 10, 2010

skateboards and more
6243 rock avenue
detroit, michigan 48201

To whom it may concern:

I am returning my skateboard for repair. it is still under warranty. please repair it and return the skateboard to the address above as soon as possible.

sincerely,

wesley diaz

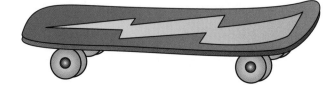

FITNESS FLASH: Hop on your left foot 10 times.

* See page ii.

PLACE STICKER HERE

Congruent figures have the same size and shape. Decide if each pair of figures is congruent. Circle the correct answer.

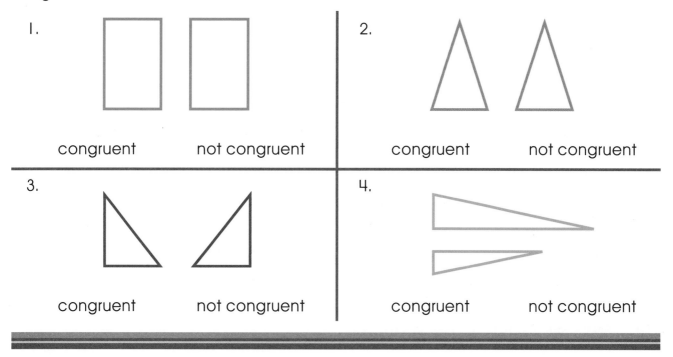

1. congruent   not congruent

2. congruent   not congruent

3. congruent   not congruent

4. congruent   not congruent

Separate each run-on sentence into two sentences. Use correct capitalization and punctuation to write the new sentences.

5. Raven has a new backpack it is green and has many zippers.

    _____

6. Katie borrowed my pencil she plans to draw a map.

    _____

7. Zoe is outside she is on the swings.

    _____

8. Zack is helping Dad Elroy is helping Dad too.

    _____

DAY 15

Circle the measurement from the parentheses that correctly completes each sentence.

9. A bathtub could hold up to (10 quarts, 10 gallons) of water.

10. A flower vase could hold up to (1 liter, 1 milliliter) of water.

11. A bike would weigh (20 grams, 20 kilograms).

12. An orange would weigh (7 ounces, 7 pounds).

13. An ear of corn would be (11 inches, 11 yards) long.

14. A new pencil would be (7 meters, 7 centimeters) long.

Underline the word from the parentheses that correctly completes each sentence.

15. There aren't (no, any) letters for you today.

16. I don't (ever, never) get to go camping.

17. Hasn't (anybody, nobody) seen my green jacket?

18. Rob bumped his head; he doesn't remember (nothing, anything).

19. I (haven't, have) never flown in a jet.

20. I don't have (no, any) work to do.

21. There is never (anything, nothing) fun to do on Saturday.

22. Can't (nobody, anybody) fix this step?

CHARACTER CHECK: Think of three things that you like about yourself. Write these characteristics on a separate sheet of paper and post it where you will see it often.

PLACE STICKER HERE

Read the story. Then, answer the questions.

Julie and Clint closed their eyes to shut out the sun's glare. As they sat on the ground, the hot July sun felt good. They could hear the wind blowing softly through the pine trees, making a kind of whispering, murmuring sound. They could hear the creek nearby making soothing, babbling sounds. They could even hear the distant screech of a hawk flying high in the sky overhead.

1. Where do you think Julie and Clint are? _____

2. What season of the year is it? _____

3. What could Julie and Clint hear? _____

_____

4. What would you like to do if you were there? _____

_____

Imagine that you are having a party to celebrate something good. Write about what you are celebrating. Then, on a separate sheet of paper, design an invitation for your party.

_____

_____

_____

_____

_____

_____

DAY 16

Add to find each sum. Regroup if needed.

5. 246
    + 129

6. 500
    + 806

7. 924
    + 289

8. 402
    + 629

9. 1,284
    + 2,629

10. 7,762
    + 1,473

11. 3,383
    + 5,007

12. 4,290
    + 2,968

13. 9,542
    + 695

14. 2,423
    + 1,932

Write an adjective in each blank to complete each sentence.

15. A _____ family moved in next door yesterday.

16. The bear has _____ , _____ fur.

17. The _____ birds woke me up this morning.

18. Her _____ , _____ balloon floated away.

Demonstrative pronouns identify specific nouns. Write the correct demonstrative pronoun (*this*, *that*, *these*, or *those*) to complete each sentence. Use *this* and *that* with singular nouns. Use *these* and *those* with plural nouns.

19. _____ book is one of my favorites.

20. Is _____ hat the one Mom wanted?

21. _____ planet is very far away.

22. _____ ducks didn't come back to the pond this year.

FACTOID: The speed of a boat is measured in units called knots.

PLACE STICKER HERE

Subtract to find each difference. Regroup if needed.

1. $\begin{array}{r} 3.01 \\ -2.42 \end{array}$	2. $\begin{array}{r} 5.41 \\ -3.77 \end{array}$	3. $\begin{array}{r} 4.71 \\ -3.82 \end{array}$	4. $\begin{array}{r} 7.27 \\ -4.19 \end{array}$	5. $\begin{array}{r} 8.48 \\ -3.99 \end{array}$
6. $\begin{array}{r} 8.47 \\ -3.58 \end{array}$	7. $\begin{array}{r} 5.02 \\ -3.21 \end{array}$	8. $\begin{array}{r} 7.04 \\ -6.67 \end{array}$	9. $\begin{array}{r} 8.46 \\ -4.57 \end{array}$	10. $\begin{array}{r} 6.03 \\ -2.77 \end{array}$

Read the story. Then, answer the questions.

Swimming Lessons

Ann and her brother took swimming lessons this summer. Because they live in the country, they took a bus to the pool. It took half an hour to get there. Their lessons were two hours long, then they rode the bus home. Even though it took a lot of time, they enjoyed it very much. By the end of the summer, they both knew how to swim well.

11. What is the best summary for this story?
    A. Ann and her brother took swimming lessons this summer.
    B. Ann and her brother rode a bus to the pool to take swimming lessons this summer. They enjoyed it and both learned how to swim.

12. Should a summary be longer or shorter than the original story?_____

13. What information should be included in the summary? _____

_____

_____

_____

DAY 17

Solve each word problem. Show your work.

14. Don is picking apples. He puts 36 apples in each box. How many apples does he put in 9 boxes?

15. Miss Brown has 25 students in her class. She wants to make 5 equal teams for a relay race. How many students will be on each team?

16. Zack has saved $9.00 toward buying a new ball. He will get $3.00 today from his father. How much more money will he need to buy the $19.95 ball?

17. Jenna saves 867 pennies in May, 942 in July, and 716 in June. How many pennies does she save in these three months?

Read each group of words. Write *S* if it is a sentence, *F* if it is a fragment, or *R* if it is a run-on sentence.

18. _____ Orangutans are rare animals.

19. _____ Live in rain forests in Borneo and Sumatra.

20. _____ They belong to the ape family along with the chimpanzees and gorillas and they are larger than most chimpanzees and smaller than most gorillas.

21. _____ Approximately three to five feet tall.

22. _____ Their arms are extremely long.

FITNESS FLASH: Hop on your left foot for 30 seconds.

* See page ii.

PLACE STICKER HERE

Where would you find the answer to each of the following questions? Write the name of the best reference from the word bank.

| globe | dictionary | encyclopedia |

1. Where is Oregon? _____

2. How do they harvest sugarcane in Hawaii? _____

3. Which syllable is stressed in the word *Utah*? _____

4. What kind of food do people eat in Mexico? _____

5. Which continent is closest to Australia? _____

6. Where is the Indian Ocean? _____

7. Who was Thomas Edison, and what did he do? _____

8. What does the word *hibernate* mean? _____

9. What are two different meanings for the word *project*? _____

The proofreading mark ^ is used to show where a word, letter, or punctuation mark needs to be added in a sentence. Use the proofreading mark ⌄ to show where commas are needed in each sentence.

10. As a bird of prey the American kestrel eats insects mice lizards and other birds.

11. Birds of prey such as hawks have hooked beaks and feet with claws.

12. Falcons are powerful fliers and they can swoop from great heights.

13. The American kestrel the smallest North American falcon is only 8 inches (20.3 cm) long.

14. "Kim let's look at this book about falcons."

Read the passage. Then, answer the questions.

Scientific Experiments

Scientists learn about the world by conducting experiments. They take careful notes about the supplies they use and the results they find. They share their findings with others, which leads to everyone learning a little more. You can do experiments too! The library has many books with safe experiments for students. You might work with balloons, water, or baking soda. You might learn about how light travels or why marbles roll down a ramp. Ask an adult to help you set up your experiment and to make sure that you are being safe. Be sure to wash your hands afterward and clean up the area. Take good notes about your work. Remember, you may be able to change just one thing the next time to get a completely different result. Most of all, do not worry if your results are different from what you expected. Some of the greatest scientific discoveries were made by mistake!

15.   What is the main idea of this passage?
  A.   Scientists learn about the world by conducting experiments.
  B.   Scientists sometimes make mistakes that lead to great discoveries.
  C.   You should always take good notes when conducting an experiment.

16.   What do scientists take notes about? _____

17.   What happens when scientists share their findings with others?

_____

18.   Where can you find information about safe experiments? _____

19.   Why should you ask an adult to help you with your experiment?

_____

20.   Should you worry if you get different results? Why or why not?

_____

> **FACTOID:** It takes almost 250 Earth years for Pluto to complete one orbit around the sun.

PLACE STICKER HERE

Solve each problem.

1. 25 – 5 = _____
2. 36 – 16 = _____
3. 18 – 8 = _____

4. 28 ÷ 4 = _____
5. 36 ÷ 6 = _____
6. 9 × 2 = _____

7. 11 × 11 = _____
8. 16 + 6 = _____
9. 17 + 3 = _____

10. 6 × 1 = _____
11. 18 ÷ 3 = _____
12. 10 × 3 = _____

13. 14 ÷ 7 = _____
14. 5 × 6 = _____
15. 7 × 7 = _____

The range is the difference between the largest number and the smallest number in a group. To calculate the mean (or average), add all of the numbers, then divide by the number of items. The median is the middle number that appears in a group. The mode is the number that appears most often. Use the data to answer each question.

Lengths of Whales and Dolphins

Whales	Dolphins
blue whale ....88 feet	bottle-nosed dolphin......................9 feet
humpback whale ....54 feet	rough-toothed dolphin...................8 feet
gray whale ....39 feet	Atlantic spotted dolphin ....7 feet
sperm whale ....35 feet	spinner dolphin.............................7 feet
beluga whale .... 13 feet	

16. What is the range of the data? _____

17. What is the mean of the data? _____

18. What is the median of the data? _____

19. What is the mode of the data? _____

DAY 19

Write the correct probability word from the word bank to complete each sentence.

certain	more likely	less likely	impossible

Pascal has 13 CDs in his CD case. Six CDs are rock, 2 CDs are hip-hop, 2 CDs are country, and 3 CDs are classical.

20. Pulling a classical CD from the case is _____ than pulling a rock CD from the case.

21. Pulling a rock CD from the case is _____ than pulling a country CD from the case.

22. Pulling a jazz CD from the case is _____.

23. Pascal has another case of 16 CDs, and 16 of the CDs are classical. Pulling a classical CD from the new case is _____.

Read the passage. Then, follow the directions.

In France, pancakes are called crepes. They are made with flour, eggs, and other ingredients. They are usually rolled up with different kinds of food inside. Most often, they are filled with fruit. In Mexico, pancakes made with cornmeal are called tortillas. Tortillas are filled with a mixture of foods. Tortillas can also be folded to make tacos.

On another sheet of paper, write a recipe for your favorite pancakes. Describe what you like to have on top of them.

FITNESS FLASH: Do 10 jumping jacks.

* See page ii.

PLACE STICKER HERE

Subtract to find each difference. Regroup if needed.

1. 5,042
   − 1,624

2. 2,710
   − 1,624

3. 4,200
   − 1,122

4. 7,106
   − 2,410

5. 3,340
   − 1,112

6. 9,824
   − 1,224

7. 6,831
   − 4,560

8. 7,605
   − 1,282

9. 6,351
   − 5,675

10. 8,001
    − 2,381

Adding commas between items in a series gives meaning to a sentence. Write the letter of each correctly punctuated sentence.

11. _____ Five children went on a bus to the zoo.

   A. Jeannie, Julio, John, Dennis, and Dave went together.

   B. Jeannie, Julio, John Dennis, and Dave went together.

12. _____ There are three things to eat for lunch today.

   A. We have chicken, sandwiches, carrot sticks, and soup.

   B. We have chicken sandwiches, carrot sticks, and soup.

13. _____ Ted can't find his four sisters.

   A. Mary Ellen, Shauna, Reese, and Lisa are hiding.

   B. Mary, Ellen, Shauna, Reese, and Lisa are hiding.

DAY 20

Read the passage. Then, answer the questions.

Flags

A flag tells something special about a country or a group. For example, the United States flag has 13 red and white stripes for the country's first 13 states. It has 50 white stars on a blue background to represent the current 50 states. The Canadian flag has a red maple leaf on a white background between two bands of red. The maple tree is the national tree of Canada. Canadian provinces and U.S. states also have their own flags. The state flag of Texas has a large white star on a blue background on the left and two bands of red and white on the right. The star symbolizes Texas's independence from Mexico. Because of the flag's single star, Texas is called the Lone Star State. The flag of the Canadian province New Brunswick has a gold lion on a red background above a sailing ship. The lion stands for ties to Brunswick, Germany, and to the British king. The ship represents the shipping industry.

14. What is the main idea of this passage?
    A. A flag tells something special about the country or the group it represents.
    B. Some flags have maple leaves or lions on them.
    C. Many flags are red, white, or blue.

15. What does the United States flag look like? _____

    _____

16. What does the Canadian flag look like? _____

    _____

17. Why is Texas called the Lone Star State? _____

    _____

CHARACTER CHECK: What is the hardest task that you have ever done? How did you feel when it was over? On a separate sheet of paper, write a paragraph about your experience.

Spoon Bell

How can the pitch of sound be changed?

Pitch is a property of sound. A sound's pitch is determined by the frequency of the waves that are producing it. Pitch is often described in terms of the highness or lowness of a sound.

Materials:
- 30 inches (76 cm) of string
- metal spoon
- table

Procedure:

Tie the handle of the spoon to the center of the string. Wrap the ends of the string around your index fingers.

Place the tip of each index finger in each ear. Lean over so that the spoon hangs freely. Tap the spoon against the side of a table. Listen carefully. Then, record your observations on the chart below.

Shorten the string by wrapping more of it around your fingers. Tap the spoon against the table again. Then, record your observations on the chart below.

Trial	Observations
1	
2	

Which trial was louder? _____

What's This All About?

The vibrating molecules in the spoon hit the string's molecules. The energy is transferred up the string to your ears. When the vibrations travel across a long string, they spread out and have a lower frequency and a lower pitch. When you shorten the string, the movements are more compressed. This results in a higher frequency and a higher pitch.

BONUS

Germination

What conditions affect seeds as they germinate?

Materials:

- 2 small, empty jars
- masking tape
- pencil
- scissors

- 10 radish seeds
- sheet of paper towel
- permanent marker
- water

Procedure:

Open one jar. Draw four circles on the paper towel, using the mouth of the jar as your guide. Cut out the circles.

Put one paper towel circle in the bottom of each jar. Then, put five radish seeds into each jar. Put another paper towel circle over the radish seeds in each jar. Each jar should now have a "sandwich" made of two paper towel circles and five radish seeds.

Add enough water to each jar to moisten, but not drown, the paper towel circles. If you add too much water, pour it out; the seeds will be OK. Label your jars with the pencil and the masking tape. Label one jar *warm* and the other *cold*.

Put the *cold* jar in the refrigerator. Put the *warm* jar in a warm, dark place where it will not be disturbed, such as a drawer. Check the seeds every day for four days. Record your observations on a separate sheet of paper.

In which location did the seeds germinate faster? Why do you think this is?

_____

_____

What's This All About?

Several factors affect the germination of seeds. Mainly, seeds are affected by the amount of water available and the temperature. A seed waits until ideal weather conditions exist before sprouting. Some seeds must go through a period of dormancy, or sleep, and endure severe cold before they will germinate. You can put those seeds in a freezer for six weeks so that it feels like winter to them. They will then germinate when planted.

Product Map

A product map uses symbols to show which products are produced in certain places. Below is a product map of Wisconsin. Study the map. Then, answer the questions.

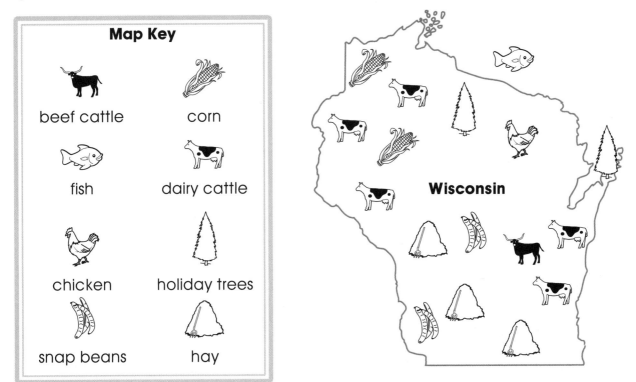

Map Key

beef cattle   corn

fish   dairy cattle

chicken   holiday trees

snap beans   hay

Wisconsin

1. What product does Wisconsin produce the most of? _____

2. Are more chickens or dairy cattle raised in Wisconsin? _____

3. Which two products are produced the least? _____

4. Judging from the map, does Wisconsin produce more livestock or crops?

    _____

5. Why might it be helpful to know where products are produced? _____

    _____

    _____

BONUS

Making a Map

Use an atlas to make a map of Africa. Draw and label the features in the list. Then, follow the directions.

Ahaggar Mountains
Atlas Mountains
Congo River
Lake Chad
Madagascar (Island)

Lake Tanganyika
Lake Victoria
Namib Desert
Nile River

Mediterranean Sea
Red Sea
Sahara Desert
Strait of Gibraltar

1. Color the deserts orange.

2. Draw brown triangles for the mountains.

3. Draw blue lines and circles for the rivers and lakes.

4. Draw a green line on the equator.

5. Draw red circles on the Tropic of Cancer and the Tropic of Capricorn.

Hemispheres

The prime meridian (0° longitude) and the meridian at 180° longitude divide Earth into two halves called the eastern hemisphere and the western hemisphere. Study the map below. Then, circle the correct hemisphere in parentheses to complete each sentence. Use an atlas or a world map if needed to help you identify each continent.

0°

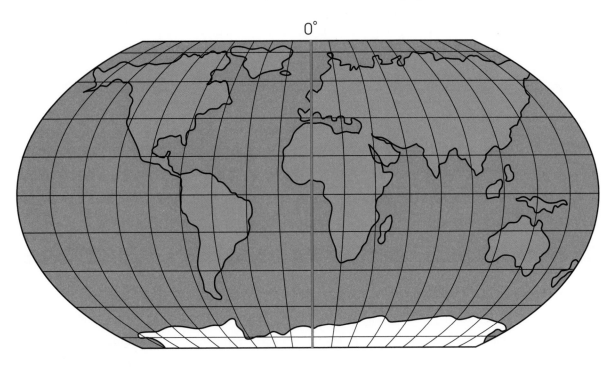

1. North America is in the (eastern, western) hemisphere.

2. Asia is mostly in the (eastern, western) hemisphere.

3. Africa is in the (eastern, western) hemisphere.

4. South America is in the (eastern, western) hemisphere.

5. Europe is in the (eastern, western) hemisphere.

6. Australia is mostly in the (eastern, western) hemisphere.

Take It Outside!

Take a notebook, a pencil, and a ruler outside. With an adult, find a garden or outdoor container garden where something is growing in groups, such as flowers, leaves, or vegetables. Locate the largest and smallest sample of each object and estimate their dimensions. Then, measure and compare each object. Continue estimating, measuring, and comparing objects until you are very close at estimating the exact answers.

You do not need a high-powered telescope to glimpse incredible sights in the night sky. With an adult, research the summer night sky to learn what stars can be seen where you live. Then, on a clear night, go outside with an adult. If you watch regularly, you might be able to see a meteor shower, a special star, or a distinctive constellation. Whatever the summer sky offers, keep a journal of your observations.

Archaeologists find and uncover objects. Then, they piece clues together to learn about the past. With your gardening gloves and a small shovel, go to an outdoor location where you have permission to dig. Dig several inches in a few different locations and examine what you find. Whether it is a quarter from 1978, an old button, or a fossil, you may be surprised by an interesting find. As you uncover the various items, consider how each object found its way into the earth. When you are finished, be sure to fill the holes you dug and clean up any mess that you made.

* See page ii.

Section I

Day I: sums; differences; I. 10; 2. 48; 3. 69; 4. 35; 5. 2; 6. 27; 7. 16; 8. 46; 9. 58; 10. 12; II. 29; 12. 69; 13. II; 14. 12; 15. 56; 16. 23; 17. 39; 18. 78; 19. B; 20. when snow hardens into ice over a long period of time; 21. A; 22. Antarctica and Greenland; 23. a lot of snow in winter and cool summers;
24. Falling ice may block paths. Glaciers can cause flooding. Icebergs may break and cause problems for ships at sea.

Day 2: I. two; 2. read; 3. paws; 4. too; 5. too; 6. Red; 7. to; 8. pause; 9.–13.

b	r	q	e	o	Ⓢ	c	r	y	10	6	X
Ⓤ	y	10	X	2	4	Ⓜ	z	I	X	a	i
6	v	0	X	8	Ⓜ	p	2	10	17	12	I
r	b	14	X	b	e	16	f	h	X	Ⓔ	s
18	X	14	7	2	p	m	n	z	58	20	s
94	86	22	2	Ⓡ	X	Ⓘ	0	24	n	x	c
26	39	3	a	d	e	28	g	Ⓢ	52	X	30
X	j	Ⓕ	k	32	y	34	4	X	t	10	36
0	n	e	n	38	o	80	98	Ⓤ	47	x	p
w	m	m	X	Ⓝ	X	14	X	c	r	e	t
q	u	v	X	X	6	w	X	40	w	X	X

14. SUMMER IS FUN; 15. 8 + 7 = 15, 7 + 8 = 15, 15 − 7 = 8, 15 − 8 = 7; 16. 9 + 8 = 17, 8 + 9 = 17, 17 − 8 = 9, 17 − 9 = 8; 17. 8 + 6 = 14, 6 + 8 = 14, 14 − 6 = 8, 14 − 8 = 6

Day 3: I. 902; 2. 1,476; 3. 770; 4. 1,133; 5. 1,031; 6. 1,223; 7. 890; 8. 880; 9. 601; 10. 1,002; II. D; 12. IN; 13. D; 14. D; 15. E; 16. E; 17. IM; 18. IN; 19. D; 20. E; 21. dis-; 22. re-; 23. dis-; 24. un-; 25. in-; 26. in-; 27. dis-; 28. un-; 29. dis-; 30. nonfiction.

Day 4: I. 16 books; 2. 8 photos; 3. 27 birds; 4. 5 tadpoles; 5. S; 6. F; 7. F; 8. S; 9. F; 10. S; II. S; 12. F; 13. S; 14. 94; 15. 50; 16. 100; 17. 368; 18. 402; 19. 675; 20. 953; 21. large; 22. dried; 23. four; 24. good; 25. six; 26. many

Day 5: I. B; 2. 776 BC, Greece; 3. wreaths of olive branches; 4. The International Olympic Committee decided that the summer and winter Olympic Games should be held in different years; 5. gold, silver, or bronze medals; 6. Host countries get a chance to show their culture to athletes, visitors, and spectators; 7. 97; 8. 132; 9. 138; 10. 167; II. 57; 12. 125; 13. 118; 14. 88; 15. 177; 16. 139; 17. softer, softest; 18. larger, largest; 19. flatter, flattest; 20. sweeter, sweetest; 21. wider, widest; 22. cooler, coolest

Day 6: I. 6.42; 2. 5.82; 3. 11.65; 4. 7.32; 5. 12.96; 6. 9.37; 7. 7.75; 8. 8.7; 9. 10.1; 10. 10.83; II. Answers will vary but may include: 4 quarters, 10 dimes, 20 nickels, 100 pennies; 12. Answers will vary but may include: 2 dimes and I nickel, 5 nickels, I dime and 15 pennies, I quarter; 13. Answers will vary but may include: 16 dimes, 6 quarters and I dime, 32 nickels; The following words should be circled: elephant, tent, Mr. Chip, team, book, California, guitar, Lake Street, Kent, strength, engine, broccoli; The following words should be underlined: sang, ate, fixed, laugh, landed, cleaned, yell, played, visited, write, jump. leap

Day 7: I. 561; 2. 800; 3. 486; 4. 150; 5. 2,021; 6. 4,011; 7. pineapple; 8. scarecrow; 9. snowstorm; 10. horseback; II. teammates; 12. 90; 13. 10; 14. 40; 15. 30; 16. 90; 17. 80; 18. 20; 19. 800; 20. 800; 21. 200; 22. 600; Last summer, we went camping in Colorado. We went hiking and swimming every day. One time, I actually saw a baby white-tailed deer with spots. We also took photos of a lot of pretty rocks, flowers, and leaves. We had a great time. I didn't want to leave.

Day 8: I. 132; 2. 107; 3. 75; 4. 195; 5. 166; 6. 109; 7. 146; 8. 122; 9. 151; 10. 126; II. 113; 12. 99; 13. nowhere, anywhere; 14. nobody, anybody; 15. no, any; 16. never, ever; 17. nothing, anything; 18. cac/tus; 19. blis/ter; 20. al/ways; 21. har/bor; 22. flow/er; 23. bas/ket; 24. o/beys; 25. Wed.; 26. Jan.; 27. Aug.; 28. Sun.; 29. Thurs.; 30. Feb.; 31. Sept.; 32. Mon.; 33. Fri.; 34. Mar.; 35. Oct.; 36. Tues.; 37. Sat.; 38. Apr.; 39. Nov.

Day 9: I. <; 2. >; 3. <; 4. >; 5. <; 6. <; 7. <; 8. <; 9. >; 10. >; II. <; 12. <; 13. tip; 14. lid; 15. happy; 16. tear; 17. tug; 18. silent; 19. mistake; 20. small; 21. C; 22. to help rescue her family and help other slaves; 23. the network of people who helped slaves escape to freedom; 24. helped move slaves to freedom; 25. struggle between northern and southern states, partially over slavery

Day 10: I. 642; 2. 582; 3. 1,165; 4. 732; 5. 1,296; 6. 937; 7. 775; 8. 870; 9. 1,010; 10. 1,083; II. 791; 12. 1,071; 13. Dogs, cats, gerbils,

and hamsters can be pets too.;
14. I am wearing blue jeans, a striped shirt, black shoes, green socks, and a baseball cap.;
15. rectangle; 16. hexagon; 17. pentagon; 18. octogon; 19. square; 20. triangle; The following words should have three lines drawn beneath the first letter: Pocahontas, Virginia, English, America, Pocahontas, Captain, John, Smith, Jamestown, Rebecca, Mr., John, Rolfe, England, King, James, Pocahontas, England, Thomas.

Day 11: 1. numb; 2. knead; 3. certain; 4. purchase; 5. sense; 6. wheat; 7. guide; 8. praise; 9. 1,033; 10. 1,333; 11. 1,324; 12. 1,164; 13. 1,610; 14. 1,133; 15. 1,272; 16. 783; 17. 601; 18. 842; The following words should have three lines drawn beneath them: July, Dear, Aunt, I've, Uncle, Your.

Day 12:

1. Make 5 equal groups.

How many are in each group? __3__

2. Make 2 equal groups.

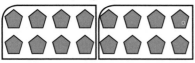

How many are in each group? __8__

3. Make 4 equal groups.

How many are in each group? __2__

4. My parents were married in Portland, Oregon, on May 1, 1999; 5. We had chicken,

potatoes, corn, gravy, and ice cream for dinner; 6. George Washington became the first U.S. president on April 30, 1789; 7. Sam was born on June 16, 1947, in Rome, Italy; 8. We saw deer, bears, elk, and goats on our trip; 9. On July 24, 1962, in Boise, Idaho, I won the big race.; 10. 312; 11. 1,617; 12. 2,436; 13. 2,142; 14. 7,332; 15. 2,592; 16. 414; 17. 2,035; 18. 1,798; 19. 3,450; 20–25. Answers will vary.

Day 13: 1. equal to; 2. more than; 3. less than; 4. equal to; 5. less than; 6. equal to; 7. less than; 8. equal to; 9. knock; 10. hopped; 11. night; 12. baby; 13. different; 14. pear; 15. dry; 16. A; 17. Puerto Rico; 18. Pittsburgh; 19. helped people in Puerto Rico; 20. an earthquake; 21. to deliver supplies

Day 14: 1. 9 days; 2. 12 people; 3. June 29; 4. 15 people; 5–19. Students should circle the words in green: 5. We <u>went on a picnic</u>; 6. A little red fox <u>ran past us</u>; 7. Some Birds <u>make nests for their eggs</u>; 8. Clowns <u>make me laugh</u>; 9. The king <u>rode a bike</u>; 10. April <u>lost her</u> house keys; 11. Lee <u>auditioned for the school play</u>; 12. We <u>started to swim</u>; 13. The frog <u>hopped onto the lily pad</u>; 14. Lions <u>live in groups called prides</u>; 15. Olivia's mom <u>baked the pie</u>; 16. Noah <u>worked in his garden</u>; 17. I <u>finished the book yesterday</u>; 18. Mom and I <u>rode our horses</u>; 19. My brother <u>went to the park</u>; 20. 43; 21. 9; 22. 7; 23. 54; 24. 13; 25. 10; 26. 29; 27. 7; 28. 18; 29. 16; 30. is; 31. are; 32. am; 33. are; 34. am; 35. are; 36. is

Day 15: 1. 7 tubes; 2. 4 baskets; 3. 3 teachers; 4. 8 tickets; 5. jazz, They are instruments; 6. tire, They are tools; 7. dog, They are birds; 8. Moon, They are planets; 9. peach, They are vegetables; 10. lazy, They are flowers; 11. 3.66; 12. 14.76; 13. 2.16; 14. 11.64; 15. 4.33; 16. 12.23; 17. 8.90; 18. 2.34; 19. 6.01; 20. 3.28; 21. will cook; 22. will visit; 23. will go; 24. will read; 25. will show

Day 16: 1.–11. Answers will vary but may include: 1. saddest; 2. action; 3. direction; 4. safest/safety; 5. dirtiest; 6. hungriest; 7. invention; 8. preparation; 9. happiest; 10. heaviest; 11. honesty; 12. are; 13. is; 14. are; 15. is; 16. is; 17. are; 18. is; 19. are; 20. 547, 496, 325, 261; 21. 793, 779, 746, 733; 22. 596, 579, 499, 488; 23. 964, 946, 649, 496; 24. 647, 674, 746, 764; 25. 353, 503, 530, 550; 26. 488, 499, 579, 940; 27. 496, 649, 946, 964

Day 17: 1–4. Answers will vary; 5. -est, sad; 6. -est, hungry; 7. -tion, prepare; 8. -tion, invent; 9. -y, taste; 10. -ty, certain; 11. -ty, loyal; 12. -tion, direct; 13. -tion, suggest; 14. -est, lovely; 15. -est, sure; 16. B; 17. the main character of the Anne of Green Gables series; 18. She lived with her grandparents and went to school in a one-room schoolhouse; 19. when she was 17; 20. It was a best-seller. Two films and at least seven TV shows have been made from it; 21. to see where Anne Shirley grew up

Day 18: 1. 80; 2. 105; 3. 84; 4. 96; 5. 104; 6. 94; 7. 76; 8. 95; 9. 76; 10. 180; 11. hatched; 12. looked; 13.

used; 14. breathed; 15. changed; 16. started; 17. flattened; 18. vanished; 19. disappeared; 20. hopped; 21–23. Answers will vary; 24. / (slash); 25. first, last; 26. planes; 27. hippo; 28. sub; 29. phone; 30. photo

Day 19: 1. C; 2. The ropes sometimes broke; 3. pull the elevator back up if the cables broke; 4. 1853, New York Crystal Palace Exhibition; 5. the Eiffel Tower and the Empire State Building; 6. They continued to sell Otis's design; 7. 7; 8. 14; 9. 47; 10. 29; 11. 18; 12. 49; 13. 19; 14. 66; 15. 46; 16. 66; Answers will vary.

Day 20: 1. 17,024; 2. 15,255; 3. 10,990; 4. 188; 5. 125; 6. 1,948; 7. 15,807; 8. 2,061; 9. 17,066; 10. 14,654; 11. L; 12. A; 13. L; 14. L; 15. A; 16. A; 17. A; 18. A; 19. A; 20. A; 21. L; 22. L; 23. A; 24. L; 25. 42; 26. 31; 27. 34; 28. 31; 29. 10; 30. 11; 31. 23; 32. 11; 33. 12; 34. 10; 35. 14; 36. 20; 37. B; 38. B; 39. A; 40. A; 41. B

Coffee Filter Chromatography: 1. The ink spread up the coffee filter strips; 2. The inks separated into different colors; 3. Answers will vary.

Speed Racer: 1. The higher the ramp, the faster the object traveled; 2. Answers will vary; 3. It rolls faster.

Prime Lines: 1. 0°; 2. W; 3. E; 4. Students should trace the prime meridian.

Map Scale: 1. 500 km; 2. 175 km; 3. 550 km; 4. 900 km

Physical Features of North America: 1. E; 2. H; 3. F; 4. J; 5. C; 6. D; 7. G; 8. I; 9. B; 10. A

Section II

Day 1: 1. 586; 2. 582; 3. 1,382; 4. 1,441; 5. 1,207; 6. 1,060; 7. 1,007; 8. 974; 9. 1,089; 10. 1,351; Answers will vary; 11. "Where is the big beach ball?" asked Jeff.; 12. Ilene exclaimed, "That is a wonderful idea!"; 13. "Come and do your work," Grandma said, "or you can't go with us."; 14. "Yesterday," said Ella, "I saw a pretty robin in the tree by my window."; 15. "I will always take care of my pets," promised Theodore.; 16. Rachel said, "Maybe we should have practiced more."; 17. Dr. Jake asked, "How are you, Pat?"

Day 2: 1. green rhombus; 2. (2,2); 3. the purple triangle should be circled; 4. the pink rectangle and the red circle should be connected; The following words should be written under *Common Nouns*: dog, ocean, class, holiday, boat, beans, apple; The following words should be written under *Proper Nouns*: Monday, Main Street, November, Mr. Brown, July, Rex, North Carolina; 5. B; 6. C; 7. two; 8. cent; 9. to; 10. sent; 11. too; 12. scent

Day 3: 1. 6.26; 2. 2.40; 3. 2.44; 4. 11.52; 5. 4.13; 6. 797; 7. 933; 8. 9; 9. 100; 10. 1,150; 11–20. Students should circle the words in orange: 11. a <u>bed</u>; 12. The <u>movie</u>; 13. an <u>umbrella</u>, the <u>rain</u>; 14. a <u>leak</u>; 15. the <u>sun</u>; 16. an <u>apple</u>, a <u>sandwich</u>; 17. the <u>nails</u>, an <u>egg carton</u>; 18. The <u>books</u>, the <u>shelf</u>; 19. a <u>blue whale</u>, the <u>ocean</u>; 20. The <u>elephant</u>; 21. wonderful; 22. warm; 23. worried; 24. who; 25. where; 26. weigh; 27. want; 28. won't

Day 4: 1. $\overrightarrow{AB}$; 2. $\overleftrightarrow{GH}$; 3. $\overline{LM}$; 4. $\overleftrightarrow{CD}$; 5. $\overrightarrow{UT}$; 6. $\overrightarrow{WX}$; 7. pears; 8. seem; 9. flour; 10. right; 11. won; 12. dough; 13. B; 14. A; 15. C; 16. C; 17. A

Day 5: 1. 3:30; 2. 55 minutes; 3. 4:00; 4. 3:45; 5. the; 6. an; 7. a, a; 8. the; 9. a; 10. a; 11. the; 12. a; 13. an; 14. 13,011; 15. 1,410; 16. 166; 17. 1,350; 18. 239; 19. 180; 20. 1,305; 21. 12,077; 22. 24,672; 23. 8,696; 24–31. Students should circle the words in orange: 24. usually <u>go</u>; 25. <u>drive</u> slowly; 26. often <u>begins</u>; 27. <u>plays</u> loudly; 28. <u>cheers</u> excitedly; 29. <u>pass</u> near; 30. <u>decorated</u> beautifully; 31. never <u>see</u>

Day 6: 1. 8, 16, 12, 18, 14; 2. 21, 15, 6, 12, 24; 3. 40, 32, 16, 28, 24, 36; 4. 45, 10, 30, 25, 35, 20; 5. pictures; 6. market; 7. cottage; 8. quarter; 9. pennies; 10. circus; 11. bell; 12. curtains; 13. chatter; 14. 6; 15. 5; 16. 12; 17. 9; 18. 7; 19. 5; 20. 8; 21. 4; 22. read; 23. knew; 24. told; 25. said; 26. heard; 27. bought; 28. found; 29. ate; 30. built

Day 7: 1. The line should be drawn through 28, 32, and 18; 2. The line should be drawn through 16, 22, and 72; 3. The line should be drawn through 71, 82, and 98; 4. The line should be drawn through 63, 25, and 61; 5. The line should be drawn through 100, 206, and 200; 6. The line should be drawn through 79, 20, and 90; 7. make; 8. rolled; 9. enjoyed; 10. helps; 11. places; 12. painted; 13. give; 14. I rode down the hill on a bike.; 15. My mom and I planted a garden in our backyard.; 16. All of the animals

ANSWER KEY

braced themselves when the elephants sneezed.; 17. Cory pulled a wagon full of bottles.; 18. I closed my book and went to bed.; 19. 15, 18, 21, 27; 20. 30, 36, 42, 54, 60; 21. 28, 32, 36, 40, 48; 22. 21, 18, 15, 12, 6; 23. 92, 90, 88, 84, 82

Day 8: 1. 60; 2. 20; 3. 10; 4. -10; 5. 5; 6.30; 7. 6; 8. 2, 3; 9. 2, 4; 10. 17; 11. 8; 12. 7; 13. 1; 14. 5; 15. 9; 16. 4; 17. 7; 18. 3; 19. 4; 20. 11; 21. 2

Day 9: 1. 3; 2. 2; 3. 5; 4. 3; 5. 4; 6. 4; 7. 5; 8. 6; 9. correct; 10. correct; 11. careful; 12. correct; 13. garden; 14. babies; 15. correct; 16. correct; 17. movie; 18. correct; 19. He lets people borrow his skateboard, and he can be counted on; 20. Yes, because she takes turns and is fair; 21. Answers will vary but may include going to school, going to summer camp, going to the recreation center, skateboarding, and riding bikes; 22. Answers will vary.

Day 10: 1. 117 pounds; 2. 272 marbles; 3. 122 balls; 4. 7 cards; 5–8. Answers will vary; 9. 394; 10. 663; 11. 258; 12. 28; 13. 226; 14. 312; 15. 2,688; 16. 3,589; 17. 2,835; 18. 5,464; 19. sang; 20. told; 21. brought; 22. worn; 23. took

Day 11: 1. 14,485; 2. 17,723; 3. 2,074; 4. 15,908; 5. 7,658; 6. 1,244; 7. 18,621; 8. 19,739; 9. 15,878; 10. 22,319; 11. wolves; 12. shelves; 13. hooves; 14. children; 15. wives; 16. leaves; 17. 10,368; 18. 5,392; 19. 11,742; 20. 36; 21. 226; 22. 312; 23. 2,688; 24. 3,589; 25. 2,835; 26. 5,464; 27. positive;

28. magnify; 29. follow; 30. urgent; 31. nurse; 32. twirl; 33. return; 34. worse

Day 12: 1. 123.34; 2. 139.58; 3. 78.86; 4. 128.57; 5. 145.63; 6. 111.15; 7. 129.52; 8. 96.71; 9. 84.91; 10. 133.13; 11. I; 12. E; 13. B; 14. C; 15. D; 16. A; 17. H; 18. F; 19. G; 20. give the sunglasses to the girl; 21. Answers will vary; 22. octopus; 23. crocodile; 24. cottage; 25. umbrella; 26. opposite; 27. desert

Day 13: 1. obtuse; 2. acute; 3. obtuse; 4. right; 5. we're; 6. weren't; 7. wasn't; 8. wouldn't; 9. they have; 10. should not; 11. they will; 12. I would/I had; 13. B; 14. Empty the package into a microwave-safe bowl; 15. water, milk, oatmeal, microwave-safe bowl, spoon, measuring cup; 16. B; 17. re-; 18. un-; 19. re-; 20. un-; 21. re-

Day 14: 1. 170; 2. 260; 3. 641; 4. 243; 5. 262; 6. 366; 7. 67; 8. 744; 9. 138; 10. 203; 11–15. Answers will vary; 16. Chapter 1; 17. page 40; 18. page 57; breakfast, backpack, classroom, playground, homework

Day 15: 1. 45 seeds; 2. 18 nickels; 3. $20.90; 4. 61 children; 5. apple; 6. The pineapple should be circled; 7. A peach should be drawn; 8. strawberry; 9. (1,1); 10. A square should be drawn around the grapes; 11–16. Answers will vary.

Day 16: 1. $1.46; 2. $3.55; 3. $0.93; 4. $1.66; 5. Penny's dog Coco likes to eat special snacks.; 6. Oliver Owl is teaching Owen Owl to fly.

Day 17: 1. cm; 2. m; 3. cm, cm; 4. km; 5. km; 6. m; 7. m; 8. km; 9. umbrella; 10. Juan; 11. Amira and Becca; 12. Rachel; 13. toy; 14. bus; 15. 5, 3, 15; 16. 7, 4, 28; 17. 5, 1, 5; 18. 2, 3, 6; 19. Brooke will stay and tell Ms. Havel what happened; 20. Answers will vary.

Day 18: 1. 2; 2. 5; 3. 4; 4. 6; 5. 2; 6. 2; 7. 1; 8. 1; 9. 3; 10. 9; 11. 7; 12. 9; 13. 7; 14. 5; 15. 7; 16. 2; 17. 6; 18. 8; 19–27. Answers will vary; Earth, plant, Plants, oxygen, sunlight, heat; 28. cent; 29. alter; 30. error; 31. afraid; 32. sofa; 33. present; 34. connect; 35. finish; 36. jewel

Day 19: 1. 12; 2. 42; 3. 21; 4. 33; 5. 18; 6. 55; 7. 36; 8. 91; 9. 32; 10. 28; 11. 32; 12. 10; 13. 566; 14. 54; 15. 570; weekends, outside, doghouse, backyard, butterfly, nighttime; 16–21. Students should divide each shape as directed; The following words should be written under *Compound Words*: buttermilk, airplane, snowstorm, football, daylight; The following words should be written under *Words with Prefixes or Suffixes*: selection, replanted, sleepless, peaceful, unpacked.

Day 20: 1. A; 2. A lot of rain falls quickly and fills the streets faster than they can drain; 3. It could be swept away; 4. listen to radio or TV news reports; 5. if the newscaster tells you to move to higher ground; 6. listen to news reports to find out when you can return home and when the water from your tap will be safe to drink; 7. 5:10; 8. 1:40; 9. 10:42; 10. 4:25; 11. 4:10; 12. 4:55; 13. 5:20; 14. weightless; 15. thoughtful; 16. appointment

Separating Salt and Pepper: heterogeneous

Lines of Latitude: 1. 0; 2. N; 3. S; 4. Students should trace the equator.

Latitude and Longitude:
1. Calgary; 2. Denver; 3. Boston; 4. Charleston; 5. Montreal; 6. Salt Lake City; 7. San Francisco

Coat of Arms: Drawings will vary.

Section III

Day 1: 1. 750 tires; 2. 2,250 tires; 3. go shopping for new clothes; 4. Answers will vary; 5. $2.50; 6. $0.05; 7. $0.20; 8. $3.58; 9. $10.65; 10. $0.45; 11. $6.05; 12. $15.00; 13. play; 14. interest; 15. write; 16. cover; 17. spoon; 18. quick; 19. happy; 20. doubt; 21. kind; 22. cover

Day 2: 1. A; 2. a drawing that shows how different living things are connected; 3. The animals that eat the plants would not have enough food to eat; 4. B; 5. to maintain balance in the ecosystem; 6. 10; 7. 24; 8. 2; 9. 4; 10. 2; 11. 20; 12. 4; 13. 12

Day 3: 1. 15, $3 \times 5 = 15$, $15 \div 5 = 3$, $15 \div 3 = 5$; 2. 7, $21 \div 7 = 3$, $7 \times 3 = 21$, $3 \times 7 = 21$; 3. 5, $30 \div 5 = 6$, $6 \times 5 = 30$, $5 \times 6 = 30$; 4. 0; 5. $\frac{2}{11}$; 6. $\frac{1}{11}$; 7. $\frac{3}{11}$; 8. $\frac{5}{11}$; 9. yellow; 10. A; 11. radio station; 12. newsreels in movie theaters or articles in newspapers; 13. worked as a reporter in radio and then television; 14. He started interviewing important people.

Day 4: 1. 30; 2. 3rd: 90, 4th: 100; 3. math; 4. 3rd: 15, 4th: 25;

5–10. Students should circle the words in blue: 5. <u>barked</u> loudly; 6. <u>looked</u> everywhere; 7. <u>swims</u> faster; 8. <u>walked</u> slowly; 9. <u>awoke</u> early; 10. <u>play</u> outside; 11. 6; 12. 6; 13. 7; 14. 9; 15. 4; 16. 8; 17. 6; 18. 4; 19. 5; 20. 3; 21. My family visits Spring Grove, Minnesota, every year in the summer.; 22. Dear Grandpa,; 23. Yours truly,; 24. On October 9, 2009, Carolyn saw the play.; 25. My aunt and uncle live in North Branch, New York.; 26. Dear Jon,; 27. January 1, 2010; 28. Paris, Texas, is located in the northeast part of the state.

Day 5: 1. read the books about Mexico to her grandmother; 2. Answers will vary; 3. well; 4. well; 5. better; 6. better; 7. best; 8. well; 9. worse; 10. 32 cups; 11. $1,800; 12. 20 pounds; 13. 435 containers

Day 6: 1. group of people living together; 2. in the city; 3. in the country; heading, greeting, body, closing, signature; 4. B; 5. ENIAC took up 1,800 square feet and weighed 50 tons; 6. C; 7. 1947–1955; 8. a personal computer today can weigh less than two pounds (about 1 kg) and can be operated by one person at a time.

Day 7: 1. 6, 6; 2. 3, 3; 3. 8, 8; 4. 4, 4; 5. 4, 4; 6. 4, 4; 7–14. Students should circle the phrases in blue: 7. <u>The cold weather</u> caused frost to cover the windows; 8. <u>The falling snowflakes</u> made my cheeks wet and cold; 9. Snow stuck to my mittens <u>because I had made a snowman</u>; 10. The snowman melted <u>from the heat of the sun</u>; 11. <u>I swam so long in the pool</u> that I had to put

on more sunscreen; 12. Cayce missed the bus <u>because she overslept</u>; 13. <u>Because Shay watched a scary movie on TV</u>, she could not fall asleep; 14. <u>The lady was thirsty</u>, so she went to get a glass of water; 15. A; 16. C; 17. A; 18. A; 19. C; 20. B; 21. I, her; 22. This, him; 23. me; 24. us; 25. We; 26. They, us; 27. They, them

Day 8: 1. B; 2. It is easy to get from one point in a city to another; 3. A; 4. after a fire destroyed most of London, England; 5. Philadelphia's streets are wide, organized, and easy to walk down, and London's streets are not; 6–9. Check students' work for symmetry; 10. hard; 11. honk; 12. fingers; 13. round; 14. fly; 15. small; 16. pencil

Day 9: 1. Greg, Kipley, José, and Kira; 2. Day 1; 3. 2; 4. Naomi; 5. five; 6. He is not a new student; 7. no; 8. yes; 9. no; 10. yes; 11. no; 12. no; 13. good; 14. better; 15. best; 16. bad; 17. worst; 18. good

Day 10: 1. C; 2. The paper clip will move toward the magnet; 3. Earth has magnetic poles; 4. They will stick together; 5. They will spring apart; 6. A magnetized needle points toward Earth's magnetic north pole; 7. 1; 8. $1\frac{1}{2}$; 9. $\frac{1}{3}$; 10. $\frac{2}{3}$; 11. 1; 12. 1; 13. 1; 14. $1\frac{2}{5}$; 15. $\frac{3}{5}$; 16–20. Answers will vary.

Day 11: 1. B; 2. A; 3. A; 4. $3.39; 5. $6.41; 6. $2.89; 7. $1.06; 8. $2.89; 9. $6.28; 10. $2.09; 11. $2.11; 12. $3.89; 13. $1.89

Day 12: 1. 140; 2. 10; 3. 20; 4. 43; 5. 235; 6. 40; 7. B; 8. Answers will vary but may include: boxes and books; 9. Answers will vary but may include: lemonade and orange juice; 10. Answers will vary but may include: air and helium; 11. ice, water, steam/vapor; 12. Solids have a certain shape that is difficult to change. Liquids take the shape of the container they are in. Gases fill the space they are in.

Day 13: 1. 1; 2. 1; 3. $\frac{5}{7}$; 4. 1; 5. $\frac{2}{7}$; 6. $\frac{5}{6}$; 7. I; 8. ewe; 9. eye; 10. where; 11. you; 12. wear; 13. O; 14. O; 15. F; 16. O; 17. F; 18. F; 19. F; 20. O; 21. O

Day 14: 1. C; 2. You will have a better chance of being a healthy adult later; 3. outside of school; 4. fresh fruit; 5. go for a walk with your family; 6. It wakes it up so you can do a good job on your homework; 7. H; 8. B; 9. A; 10. C; 11. E; 12. G; 13. D; 14. F; 15. B; 16. D; 17. A; 18. F; 19. G; 20. E; 21. C; 22. H; The following words should be circled: Ninth, Street, Hillside, Maine, March, Skateboards, More, Rock, Avenue, Detroit, Michigan, To, Whom, It, May, Concern, It, Please, Sincerely, Wesley, Diaz

Day 15: 1. congruent; 2. congruent; 3. congruent; 4. not congruent; 5. Raven has a new backpack. It is green with many zippers.; 6. Katie borrowed my pencil. She plans to draw a map.; 7. Zoe is outside. She is on the swings.; 8. Zack is helping Dad. Elroy is helping Dad too.; 9. 10 gallons; 10. 1 liter; 11. 20 kilograms; 12. 7 ounces; 13. 11 inches; 14. 7 centimeters; 15. any; 16. ever; 17. anybody; 18. anything; 19. have; 20. any; 21. anything; 22. anybody

Day 16: 1. Answers will vary but may include: a forest, in the woods; 2. summer; 3. the wind blowing through the pine trees, the creek nearby, and the screech of a hawk; 4. Answers will vary; 5. 375; 6. 1,306; 7. 1,213; 8. 1,031; 9. 3,913; 10. 9,235; 11. 8,390; 12. 7,258; 13. 10,237; 14. 4,355; 15–18. Answers will vary; 19. This/That; 20. This/That; 21. That; 22. Those

Day 17: 1. 0.59; 2. 1.64; 3. 0.89; 4. 3.08; 5. 4.49; 6. 4.89; 7. 1.81; 8. 0.37; 9. 3.89; 10. 3.26; 11. B; 12. shorter; 13. Answers will vary but may include: key points, main idea, names of characters; 14. 324 apples; 15. 5 students; 16. $7.95; 17. 2,525 pennies; 18. S; 19. F; 20. R; 21. F; 22. S

Day 18: 1. globe; 2. encyclopedia; 3. dictionary; 4. encyclopedia; 5. globe; 6. globe; 7. encyclopedia; 8. dictionary; 9. dictionary; 10. As a bird of prey, the American kestrel eats insects, mice, lizards, and other birds.; 11. Birds of prey, such as hawks, have hooked beaks and feet with claws.; 12. Falcons are powerful fliers, and they can swoop from great heights.; 13. The American kestrel, the smallest North American falcon, is only 8 inches (20.3 cm) long.; 14. "Kim, let's look at this book about falcons."; 15. A; 16. the supplies they use and the results they find; 17. Everyone learns a little more; 18. library; 19. to help you set up and make sure you are being safe; 20. No, because some of the greatest scientific discoveries were made by mistake.

Day 19: 1. 20; 2. 20; 3. 10; 4. 7; 5. 6; 6. 18; 7. 121; 8. 22; 9. 20; 10. 6; 11. 6; 12. 30; 13. 2; 14. 30; 15. 49; 16. 81 feet; 17. 28.9; 18. 13; 19. 7; 20. less likely; 21. more likely; 22. impossible; 23. certain

Day 20: 1. 3,418; 2. 1,086; 3. 3,078; 4. 4,696; 5. 2,228; 6. 8,600; 7. 2,271; 8. 6,323; 9. 676; 10. 5,620; 11. A; 12. B; 13. A; 14. A; 15. It has 13 red and white stripes and 50 white stars on a blue field; 16. It has a red maple leaf on a white background between two bands of red; 17. There is a single star on the state flag that symbolizes Texas's independence from Mexico.

Spoon Bell: The second trial was louder.

Germination: the warm jar; Answers will vary.

Product Maps: 1. dairy cattle; 2. dairy cattle; 3. fish and chicken; 4. crops; 5. Answers will vary.

Making a Map: Check students' drawings against an atlas for accuracy.

Hemispheres: 1. western; 2. eastern; 3. eastern; 4. western; 5. eastern; 6. eastern

arctic	brief	broadcast
© Carson-Dellosa	© Carson-Dellosa	© Carson-Dellosa
bronze	central	choose
© Carson-Dellosa	© Carson-Dellosa	© Carson-Dellosa
communicate	compass	course
© Carson-Dellosa	© Carson-Dellosa	© Carson-Dellosa

culture

© Carson-Dellosa

degree

© Carson-Dellosa

demand

© Carson-Dellosa

describe

© Carson-Dellosa

design

© Carson-Dellosa

discuss

© Carson-Dellosa

display

© Carson-Dellosa

error

© Carson-Dellosa

exhibit

© Carson-Dellosa

follow	glacier	iceberg
© Carson-Dellosa	© Carson-Dellosa	© Carson-Dellosa
improve	industry	instant
© Carson-Dellosa	© Carson-Dellosa	© Carson-Dellosa
interview	league	magnet
© Carson-Dellosa	© Carson-Dellosa	© Carson-Dellosa

magnify	murmur	nurse
official	organize	oxygen
planet	popular	positive

property

recreation

relief

represent

rescue

return

rural

scatter

scientist

surface

© Carson-Dellosa

system

© Carson-Dellosa

twirl

© Carson-Dellosa

unusual

© Carson-Dellosa

urban

© Carson-Dellosa

urgent

© Carson-Dellosa

vapor

© Carson-Dellosa

volume

© Carson-Dellosa

worse

© Carson-Dellosa

angle	edge	face
© Carson-Dellosa	© Carson-Dellosa	© Carson-Dellosa
intersecting lines	line	line segment
© Carson-Dellosa	© Carson-Dellosa	© Carson-Dellosa
parallel lines	perpendicular lines	ray
© Carson-Dellosa	© Carson-Dellosa	© Carson-Dellosa

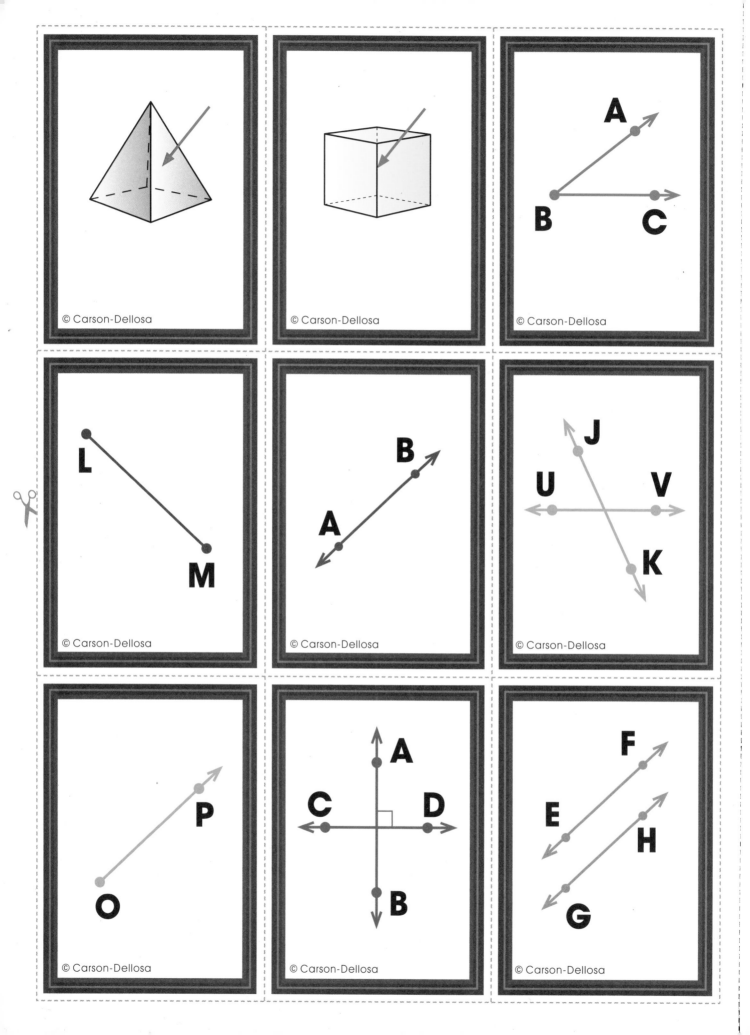

© Carson-Dellosa

A

B   C

© Carson-Dellosa

© Carson-Dellosa

L

M

© Carson-Dellosa

B

A

© Carson-Dellosa

J

U   V

K

© Carson-Dellosa

P

O

© Carson-Dellosa

A

C   D

B

© Carson-Dellosa

F

E

H

G

© Carson-Dellosa

2,4<u>8</u>5

<u>6</u>39

9,56<u>1</u>

2,7<u>4</u>9

9<u>8</u>

<u>2</u>17

<u>6</u>,513

3,<u>7</u>46

4<u>9</u>3

746

8,437

516

1,622

4,366

7,195

8,826

5,972

236

___ × 5 = 40	100 − ___ = 75	20 ÷ ___ = 10
30 ÷ ___ = 5	9 × ___ = 72	___ + 20 = 30
65 − ___ = 53	25 + ___ = 50	50 ÷ ___ = 5

$6 \times \underline{\hspace{1cm}} = 42$

$3 + \underline{\hspace{1cm}} = 19$

$24 \div \underline{\hspace{1cm}} = 3$

$44 - \underline{\hspace{1cm}} = 30$

$\underline{\hspace{1cm}} \times 9 = 63$

$\underline{\hspace{1cm}} + 22 = 38$

$25 \div \underline{\hspace{1cm}} = 5$

$3 \times \underline{\hspace{1cm}} = 18$

$60 - \underline{\hspace{1cm}} = 45$

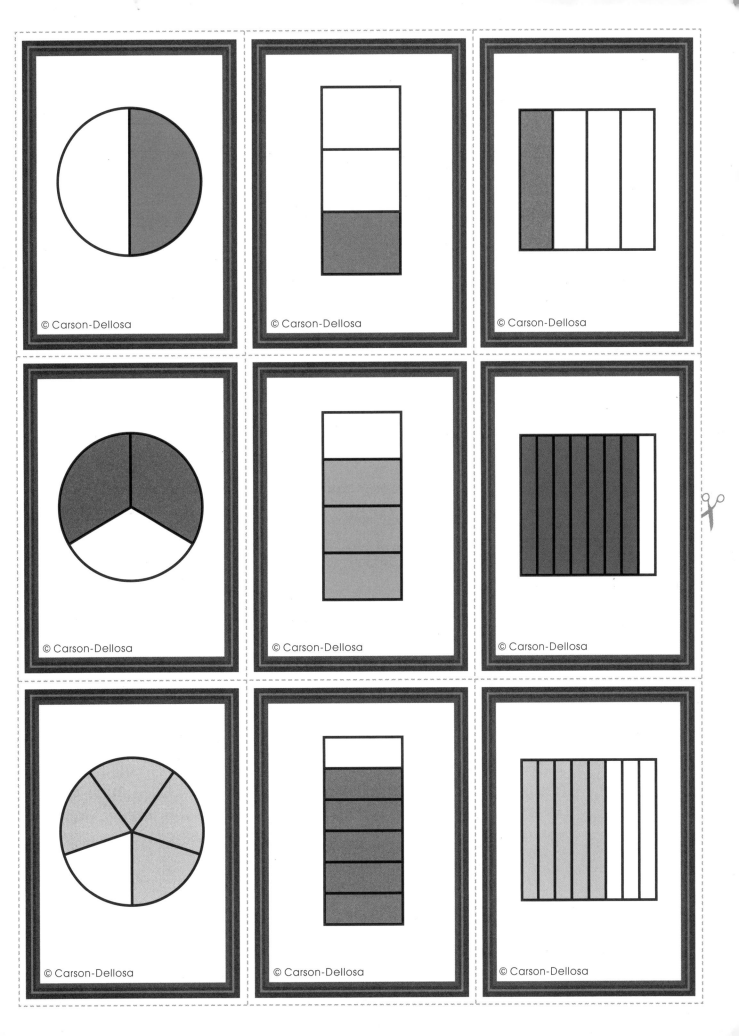

© Carson-Dellosa

© Carson-Dellosa

© Carson-Dellosa

© Carson-Dellosa

© Carson-Dellosa

© Carson-Dellosa

© Carson-Dellosa

© Carson-Dellosa

© Carson-Dellosa

one-half	one-third	one-fourth
© Carson-Dellosa	© Carson-Dellosa	© Carson-Dellosa
two-thirds	three-fourths	seven-eighths
© Carson-Dellosa	© Carson-Dellosa	© Carson-Dellosa
four-fifths	five-sixths	five-eighths
© Carson-Dellosa	© Carson-Dellosa	© Carson-Dellosa

The Original
Summer Bridge Activities™

Congratulations!

This certifies that

_____

Name

has completed **Summer Bridge Activities**™.

_____

Parent's Signature

www.carsondellosa.com